GIFTED BLACK WOMEN NAVIGATING THE DOCTORAL PROCESS

This book explores the experiences of gifted Black women doctoral graduates, featuring narratives of their challenges related to race, gender, parenthood, class, and first-generation status offering discussion on the role of community and academic support in their success.

Delivering concrete guidance on navigating the challenges of doctoral programs, this critical text draws on endarkened epistemology, recognizing the nuanced path gifted Black women walk in the academy.

Accessible and evocative, this collection highlights the role of academic and social sisterhood, supplying a much-needed contribution to the ongoing discussion around race, academic achievement, gender, and mental health.

Brittany N. Anderson is an Assistant Professor in Urban Education at the University of North Carolina at Charlotte in the Department of Middle, Secondary, and K–12 Education. Her research focuses on university-school-community partnerships that support talent development and the identification of minoritized youth in urban schools.

Shaquinta L. Richardson is an entrepreneur, consultant, and life coach for high-achieving Black women. She is a former Marriage and Family Therapist and Professor of Marriage and Family Studies. Her academic research centered on the influence of racial and gender identity on experiences of Black American women with intellectual and developmental disabilities within the family context.

GIFTED BLACK WOMEN NAVIGATING THE DOCTORAL PROCESS

Sister Insider

Edited by Brittany N. Anderson and Shaquinta L. Richardson

Designed cover image: Drs. Joan Collier & Marvette Lacy, Sista Circle Photoshoot 2017

First published 2024
by Routledge
605 Third Avenue, New York, NY 10158

and by Routledge
4 Park Square, Milton Park, Abingdon, Oxon, OX14 4RN

Routledge is an imprint of the Taylor & Francis Group, an informa business

© 2024 selection and editorial matter, Brittany N. Anderson and Shaquinta L. Richardson; individual chapters, the contributors.

The right of Brittany N. Anderson and Shaquinta L. Richardson to be identified as the authors of the editorial material, and of the authors for their individual chapters, has been asserted in accordance with sections 77 and 78 of the Copyright, Designs and Patents Act 1988.

All rights reserved. No part of this book may be reprinted or reproduced or utilized in any form or by any electronic, mechanical, or other means, now known or hereafter invented, including photocopying and recording, or in any information storage or retrieval system, without permission in writing from the publishers.

Trademark notice: Product or corporate names may be trademarks or registered trademarks and are used only for identification and explanation without intent to infringe.

Library of Congress Cataloging-in-Publication Data
Names: Anderson, Brittany N., editor. | Richardson, Shaquinta L., editor.
Title: Gifted Black women navigating the doctoral process: sister insider / edited by Brittany N. Anderson and Shaquinta L. Richardson.
Description: New York, NY: Routledge, 2024. | Includes bibliographical references and index. |
Identifiers: LCCN 2023018539 (print) | LCCN 2023018540 (ebook) | ISBN 9781032273013 (hardback) | ISBN 9781032261874 (paperback) | ISBN 9781003292180 (ebook)
Subjects: LCSH: African American women doctoral students. | African American women in higher education. | Universities and colleges–United States–Graduate work–Social aspects.
Classification: LCC LC2781 .G54 2024 (print) | LCC LC2781 (ebook) | DDC 378.1/982996073--dc23/eng/20230718
LC record available at https://lccn.loc.gov/2023018539
LC ebook record available at https://lccn.loc.gov/2023018540

ISBN: 978-1-032-27301-3 (hbk)
ISBN: 978-1-032-26187-4 (pbk)
ISBN: 978-1-003-29218-0 (ebk)

DOI: 10.4324/9781003292180

Typeset in Sabon
by Deanta Global Publishing Services, Chennai, India

CONTENTS

Foreword   *vii*
   Joy Lawson Davis, Ed.D.
Acknowledgments   *x*

  Introduction   1
  Brittany N. Anderson, Ph.D. and
  Shaquinta L. Richardson, Ph.D.

1 Navigating the Doctoral Experience as First-
  Generation, Gifted Black Women: Our Path, Our Voice   9
  Brittany N. Anderson and Shaquinta L. Richardson

2 MISUNRE: Navigating the Doctoral Journey as an
  Exceptionally Gifted Black Woman   32
  Jillian A. Martin, Ph.D.

3 It Takes a Village: Cultivating Belonging, Community,
  and Sisterhood   46
  Joan Collier, Ph.D.

4 Face Your Studies: Exploring Education, Opportunity,
  and Community as a First-Generation Immigrant   58
  Funlola G. Are, Ph.D.

5 The Evolution of My Biracial Identity through
Attending Two Predominately White Institutions 71
Megan Hicks, Ph.D.

6 All of Me: Centering *Homeplace* in Personal and
Professional Reflections of Becoming a Blackgirl
Motherscholar 83
Taryrn T.C. Brown, Ph.D.

7 Truth Be Told: Testimonies of A Black STEM Health
Scholar -Wife- Mother 99
Miranda Hill, Ph.D.

8 Navigating the Doctoral Process While Experiencing
Tragedy 111
Elizabeth Farrah Louis, Ph.D.

9 Imagining a New Thing through Active Disruption:
Tools to Center Black Aliveness and Wholeness for
Black Women in Doctoral Programs 122
*Shaquinta L. Richardson, Ph.D. and
Brittany N. Anderson, Ph.D.*

Afterword: Black Gifted Women Journeying—*Together* 131
Chonika Coleman-King, Ph.D.

About the Editors 134

About the Contributors 136

Index 141

FOREWORD

Joy Lawson Davis, Ed.D.

"To find a space where I can be whole." Such is the collective affirmation of the highly gifted female scholars whose chapters appear in this text. These young Black women, whose lived stories are so familiar to some of us and not familiar at all to others, share the psychological, mental, and spiritual toll of being Black, gifted, and female in this Nation's institutions of higher education. In this bound-to-be-a-classic text, the authors tell their backstories. They attest to the challenges but also describe the qualitative traits that make them among a population that are 68% of terminal degree holders in the nation (National Center for Education Statistics, 2022). These stories give us a glimpse into the daily experiences of these scholars, some bittersweet, others enlightening, filled with joy, and then still others unbelievably disheartening. In a nation that should be proud to nurture its highly gifted, these erudite scholars regularly faced a lack of support that, were it not for their remarkable resilience, would have driven them to give up on their dreams, leaving their well-earned positions as doctoral-level Black female students.

Research states that the most highly educated population in our nation are Black females (NCES, 2022). What this number does not indicate are the conditions faced by this highly educated population seeking to acquire the resources and encouragement they need to accomplish their goals as terminal degree program completers. The Black women authors featured in this text hail from a wide variety of communities, most as first-generation terminal degree holders. Universities that typically have reputations for providing the highest level of scholarly life for all their students often have little knowledge of what it means to be Black, gifted, and female. The authors here are like other Black female scholars who so often feel invisible, marginalized, and ignored on their campuses. What they found in each other as intellectual and social peers replaced what was lacking otherwise.

This text reminds other gifted Black women who sometimes experience "imposter syndrome" that you are not alone. For those who know what it feels like to be "miseducated," you will find your story here as well. The stress of the blessings and burdens of race ring like a clarion's call in their stories. Originating from Black families who may know what is best, but have little experience with walking the hallowed halls of our Nation's institutions, these women walked gently, but boldly, in structures built on the backs of their ancestors. Each step reminiscent of a story of their enslaved family members who reluctantly, but artistically created buildings where chains had to be broken and doors opened.

The supernatural strength that has served the Black community well across generations comes to life in the pages of this text. As a reader, you can almost hear the mothers, fathers, older siblings, aunts, grandparents, and neighbors repeatedly encouraging and nurturing their children to be the best, to never let anyone tell you where you do not fit, or what you are not capable of. These family members also remind them to never let anyone take away from you what we have given you here in this house, this neighborhood, this church, and this community. That same community who celebrated with your family upon receiving awards, certificates, and ribbons earlier in your schooling. The community that watched you "be the one" who could "show the others" who we really are as a people. Show that being Black and gifted is nothing new. Those ancestors before you and many to come after just like you, bright, talented, and Black, filled with hope, perseverance, resilience, and ingenuity that defy all the odds against you.

Academe needs to hear and respect your stories too. Academe needs to work harder to seek out the talent in the Black community and provide the foundation and mountaintop experiences that we all so justly deserve. We belong at the top: we are the top. When we are given the opportunity to see others like us who have historically paved the stony road that we later must trod, we show ourselves to be more than worthy. Our scholarship stands shoulder to shoulder and often above that of our non-Black peers. Our scholarship gives insight into a world where persistence, grit, resilience, and creativity are not the exception, but the norm. Our scholarship reveals the very best of who we are and can be as human beings. Once given access, our gifts manifest as unique diamonds that have not crumbled in the darkness, but grew and crystallized until we came from the darkness into the marvelous light as we were meant to.

The full scope of stories in this unique text provides the "first-person" view from the spirits of highly-gifted Black women in a way that has not yet been shared in gifted education literature. As such, this text will contribute to the design of innovative instructional and support pedagogies that will help generations of Black, gifted women and other gifted young people of color for generations to come. What has been revealed here are the "backstories" of the dynamic, heretofore misunderstood strength of Black families. Some were led by miseducated Black matriarchs who possess the will, creativity, and spiritual prowess of generations of a people who were oppressed, enslaved, and repeatedly brutalized. I firmly believe that this text is destined to become a classic, of uniquely lasting value for generations to come.

It has been one of the honors of my career to share this foreword. I am trusting that this book will do what it is intended to do ~ cast a blinding light into the lives of Black, gifted female scholars, their families, and the communities from whence they come so that others will learn and increase their level of true understanding of the diamonds waiting to be nurtured in schools across the nation.

JLD, 10.19.2022.

ACKNOWLEDGMENTS

I first want to thank the original and ultimate sister in my life who sparked my interest and focus on the importance of sisterhood, my big sister Tarah. You continue to be my rock and inspiration through every journey I have ever taken. To my amazing wife, who never lets me doubt myself and shows me what unwavering love looks like in action, I thank you for supporting me through this process, even when you had no idea what was going on. I am grateful for my mother, my grandmother, and all the women who raised me including my aunts, most of whom are now ancestors. I continue to gain from you while working towards a world I wish you could have seen and experienced. One where you could rest on this side. To my niece and nephews who motivate me to live a life of freedom and joy so you may know it is possible for you. Auntie loves you.

To the women in this book, contributors, and those referenced in spirit, I literally would not be here without you. Many of you held me up, pushed me, challenged me, encouraged me, and literally fed me when I needed it. I will forever be grateful. Brittany, I am consistently in awe of your beautiful mind and spirit. We cooked this up in the corner of a dining hall during a writing session and look what that moment became. It has been an honor to create what is essentially a love letter to our Black sisters with you. You're stuck with me Sis!

Black girls! May you create joy, may you know peace, and may you continue to believe in freedom for us all!

—Shaquinta L. Richardson

First and foremost, I want to thank the divine Author and finisher of my faith, who has uniquely molded my gifts and journey. I am who I am because of my village, which molded my experiences and continue to pour into me: My family. To my grandmothers, great-grandmothers, and extended family that instilled a love of storytelling, historical legacies, understanding of place, and experiential learning, I am forever thankful. To my Mama, Sandra Lakey, your unwavering support and fierce spirit is what I continue to carry with me. You trudged through the darkness, to ensure I had a safe place and space for my talents to unfold, and for that, I am truly grateful. To my niece, Brooklyn, and my younger brother, Draylon, I hope that I always serve as a place for you to imagine the possibilities. A special acknowledgment to my precious uncle, James Otis "Chip" Anderson, in his death, thank you for the love and support.

To my girlfriends and sister-scholars, I am a more thoughtful and reflective scholar, practitioner, and most importantly, friend, because of the ways you continue to hold me accountable in love, laughter, and prayer. This journey would not have been the same without you; it was with you I found safety, community, and sources of joy during so many times of transition, grief, and triumph. Your brilliance, giftedness, and unbounded talents are what the world needs. I am nothing without my community. Shaquinta, GIRL! I could not have done this without you, and it was amazing to see this grow from ideation to a product of love, learning, and growth. A special shoutout to all my mentors that continue to sow seeds of encouragement, wisdom, and freedom dreaming, I am beyond grateful for you.

Lastly, I want to thank all the gifted Black girls and women around the world that continue to inspire me through all the obstruction.

—Brittany N. Anderson

We offer a special thank you to Joy Davis and Kiarra Wigfall for their efforts in making sure this text was suitable for gifted Black women navigating doctoral programs. In addition, thank you to all the peer reviewers that provided substantive feedback to ensure each chapter provided relevant information to Black women in doctoral programs.

INTRODUCTION

*Brittany N. Anderson, Ph.D. and
Shaquinta L. Richardson, Ph.D.*

Reimagining the Gifted Gaze for Gifted Black Women

When the shared idea of compiling an edited text emerged during the last year of our doctoral programs, the primary goal was to explicate the ways we collectively acquired an understanding of institutional spaces and sisterhood, and from that, built community with other Black women to navigate the process. We still hold that sentiment as one of the tenets of this text; because together, we cried, laughed, learned, unlearned, healed, and found ourselves in this space. However, five-plus years post-graduation, we quickly found it was exponentially more than unpacking how to develop a collective, but a critical rendering of our embodied, endarkened experiences as gifted Black women. This work went beyond the scope of the doctoral program, beyond the simple attribution of being labeled gifted-identified and high-achieving. Our comprehensive perception was more than a proliferation of "making it" and writing within the white gaze of gifted or higher education. Following the blazing trail of Dillard's (2012) assertion, "By becoming all of myself, I can live not into the smallness of the world's expectations, but into the greatness of the true names You've given to me" (p. 10), we charged forth, owning our names, and creating our own understanding of the gifted label.

The evolution of this book mirrors the evolving nature of our lives. Although we have lived in these bodies our entire lives, truly nuancing the

DOI: 10.4324/9781003292180-1

nature of what it meant to be a gifted Black woman struck us on varying levels, and these nuances were mediated in our respective career paths. We unpacked what it truly meant "to be at home with myself" (Boylorn, 2016), and used our narratives and experiences as praxis to further disrupt the narrowed lens of Black womanhood being framed through resilience, success, and in gifted education's case, "invisibility." To unpack our endarkened experiences, we focused on the central question: "What does it mean to be a gifted Black woman?"

To anchor this question, we chose to situate this work through an endarkened lens. The Endarkened Feminist Epistemology (EFE) provides a stimulating reworking of traditional feminist conceptualizations, through language, that has unrelentingly commissioned Black women and girls as a homogeneous group, one with and without differences (Boylorn, 2016; Dillard, 2012; Evans-Winters & Love, 2015). An endarkened perspective embodies a distinguishable difference in the ethnological perspective that is located at the intersection of the culturally constructed socializations of race, gender, and other identities, and the historical and contemporary contexts of oppression and resistance for African-American women (Dillard, 2012). Endarkened Feminist Epistemology encourages the authentic understanding of the sacredness that exists within relationships among Black women in the endarkened spaces of Black womanhood (Dillard, 2012). Using an Endarkened Feminist Epistemology also helps to further understand the lived experiences of Black women and girls by merging their duality, welcoming them to represent who they are in spaces where the expectation of others might suggest otherwise, and helping others become more culturally responsive to their changing needs at various levels of educational spaces (Evans-Winters & Love, 2015). This epistemological understanding grounded our narratives as gifted Black women, transcending the historical, limiting knowledge of gifted and talented scholarship, and moving the traditional framing around K–12 settings. It was incredibly important to examine the gifted/high-achieving label through the lens of Black women, writing our own stories. Because of the storied history and legacy of the gifted field, we wanted to examine the complexities of their journeys to obtain a doctoral degree.

In this book, we aimed to situate our narratives through a Blackgirl [one word] perspective (Boylorn, 2016), rather than presenting fragmented perspectives of our doctoral experience alone. We found that we had to provide more contextual knowledge to our narratives, anchoring our ways of knowing and doing prior to the doctoral experience (Boylorn, 2016), because these previous experiences and survival practices followed us into these programs. We did not simply "arrive" to a space of understanding the varied ways our intersecting identities shaped the doctoral journey. Our different, but often eerily similar K–16 experiences—despite having varied social-class, and family socialization—of being a Black woman navigating spaces as high-achieving/gifted unearthed new dimensions of us understanding our identities. As editors, the critical reflections shared, fortified our insights from these experiences to create a space of bridging practice-to-theory. Communing and learning with these brilliant women inspired me (Anderson) to establish a research agenda around the ethnographic experiences of gifted Black women and use these renderings to create programming and practices to support gifted/high-achieving Black girls in K–12 settings. Experiences with these women assisted me (Richardson), to use my degree and practice to support gifted/high-achieving Black women through therapy and coaching services to deconstruct the day-to-day effects of our experiences and reconstruct a more liberated, embodied future.

The women in this text offer their voices to illuminate the multifaceted, intersectional nature of their lives. Our shared vision for this text was for it to be accessible to all; therefore, the women in this text narrate their stories in an authentic voice that honors their academic journey and creative expression. The confounded layers of our lived experiences are presented here, yet we recognize there are so many other narratives associated with being a gifted Black woman (Anderson & Martin, 2018). This contribution to educational scholarship aims to shed light on some of the intersections of gifted Black womanhood: Exceptionally gifted, first-generation American, first-generation college graduates, and biracial identities. In addition to the intersecting identities, we extrapolated the associated interpretations of gifted Black women navigating the doctoral journey during motherhood, marriage, and global tragedy. Lastly, we examined pathways to establish a sense of belonging in predominantly white institutions and spaces.

The State of Black Women in Doctoral Programs

The experiences of Black girls and women are at the paradoxical juxtaposition of oppression and achievement in the educational sector. Despite the academic achievements of Black women, there is still limited scholarship and empirical research on the processes and explanation of these contradictory experiences, in addition to the navigation of said experiences. Black women's attainment in higher education has increased dramatically since the 1970s, and this increase surpasses women in other racial groups (Esnard & Cobb-Roberts, 2018; NCES, 2022). Black women continue to hold the highest percentage of degrees in this country (NCES, 2017, 2022). Even with the increase in educational attainment, until recently, Black girls and women in current educational/social science literature have largely been missing, particularly in gifted education scholarship. However, there are still too few theoretical models to understand the experiences of Black girls and women across educational settings from a strengths-based perspective.

Black women who choose to enter higher education face barriers to full promotion and success due to widespread systematic racism on college campuses; in addition, there is a lack of representation of Black women in faculty and staff positions on university campuses who could act as role models and/or provide support for students (Hughes & Howard-Hamilton, 2003). For context, of the 176,485 tenured full professors in public and private institutions in the United States, only 2.33 percent are Black women (Esnard & Cobb-Roberts, 2018; Pittman, 2010). The visibility of Black women professors in higher education has been an issue of concern for researchers, feminists, and higher education administrators in the United States (Davis et al., 2011; Esnard & Cobb-Roberts, 2018; Evans, 2007). There has been a relative improvement for Black women earning more doctoral degrees and entering the academy as faculty, but they continue to be underrepresented in the higher ranks of academia and are promoted at a slower rate than their white counterparts (Esnard & Cobb-Roberts, 2018; Evans, 2007; Griffin et al., 2013).

To be a Black woman is to experience racialized sexism and a sense of "invisibility" on a daily basis (Collins, 1986, 2013). As an outcome of the varied gendered racism, Black women become "superinvisible" because of latent experiences associated with gender, race, and other identities in educational literature, pushing their experiences further into the margins (Chavous & Cogburn, 2007; Collins, 2013; Gholson, 2016; Haynes et al., 2016; Patton et al., 2016). However, when visible, some experiences are misrepresented, or experiences are overemphasized as "superachievers" in comparison to Black men (Chavous & Cogburn, 2007). Haynes et al. (2016) found that in their doctoral programs, they unknowingly had adopted a master narrative that was rooted in racist and sexist ideology, through a series of academic transactions they experienced in K–12 classrooms as Black girls. Franklin (1999) found that when Black men and women perceive their treatment by white people as racially motivated, feelings of indivisibility can intensify. Therefore, there has to be intentionality, a strong knowledge base, and purposeful mechanisms in how Black women and girls are mentored, challenged, and nurtured in educational spaces, particularly in doctoral programs. According to Esnard and Cobb-Roberts (2018),

Black women are valued for their diversification of the educational environment, in terms of both race and gender, but they seem to be penalized for that very same attribute and are further expected to fill a huge void although occupying limited space in numbers.

(p. 11)

Because of these circumstances, there is a strong need for an intersectional analysis of gifted-identified/high-ability Black women's experiences in doctoral programs. Intersectionality theory (Crenshaw, 1991) provides a basis for understanding the nuanced and unique experiences of Black girls whose identities intersect on the basis of race, gender, class, and cognitive ability (Anderson, 2020). Intersectionality allows for us to explore issues related to identity, power structures, social experience, and academic experience, connecting the praxis associated with navigating doctoral programs.

Purpose and Rationale

As a gifted education scholar (Anderson), I have continuously grappled with the field not "seeing" me, and this type of scholarship/work being othered or an afterthought. However, as I completed my doctoral studies and transitioned into a professorial position, I have found that I do not feel the need to be validated by "the field" per se, because this work is not for them. *This work is for us*, meaning Black women, Black girls, their families, and others that aim to understand our unique experiences. We are doing the work for ourselves, regardless of if it becomes a trend in educational sectors. Work focused on the needs of Black girls and women will continue to be in the margins, in terms of the empirical sense of methodology, strategies, and socially-just practices. However, what does it mean for us, meaning Black women, to actively pull this work from the margins, to create a working ecosystem around Black girlhood and womanhood in the gifted education sector? In the words of June Jordan (2007), "we are our sweet company," galvanizing our strength, brilliance, and talents to capture the journey and vision. To begin doing this, our scholarly aim has adjusted the "who" and "why," by first framing practice, then moving to theory by dreaming and reimagining spaces and trajectories based on our lived experiences.

This book includes the experiences of gifted Black women doctoral graduates from a PWI: Southeastern University. Each of the contributors attended the same institution, entering and graduating from their respective programs within a two-to-three-year time span. It is important to note there were several other Black women that were critical to our collective that do not have a chapter. We honor and acknowledge each of them for all they have contributed to our lives and understandings around gifted Black girl/womanhood. All of the contributors to this text were encouraged to craft their narratives in a voice and perspective that was unique to them. Following a first submission, each chapter was taken through a peer-review process. These experts were chosen because of their scholarship in women and gender studies, giftedness, Black girlhood and feminist praxis, and higher education. Separately, the chapters were also reviewed and went through a member-checking process from Black women doctoral students.

The text aims to provide guidance on how to navigate the nuanced challenges of doctoral programs, based on the contributors' unique experiences related to academic success, identity, relationships, and mental health. As many of us were "feeling our way in the dark," of navigating double oppression (hooks, 1984), global tragedies, and the doctoral journey, while still being able to experience joy, clarity, and support in our sister circle. This book can serve as a tool for the validation of gifted Black women's experiences navigating the academy, and a roadmap on how to successfully navigate the terrain of the doctoral process. The women highlighted in this book have managed to overcome many of these challenges by leaning on one another as sources of support, emphasizing the role of community and connection amongst Black women. Other gifted Black women can utilize the experiences and tools presented to assist them in their journey and craft their own understanding of collective agency to navigate their experiences. To those mentoring these women, use these tools and stories to reflect on your current practices. How are you untangling the web of intersectionality and why it matters in your mentorship? How are you making their experiences visible, and honoring their truths, even when it conflicts with your way of knowing? With this scholarship, we aspire to assist those that come behind us with new orientations and adaptations that serve and affirm us, while navigating processes/programs in a system of whiteness. **SPEAK YOUR GREAT NAME, GIFTED BLACK GIRL.**

In love and liberation,
Brittany N. Anderson, Ph.D.
Shaquinta L. Richardson, Ph.D.

References

Anderson, B. N. (2020). "See me, see us": Understanding the intersections and continued marginalization of adolescent gifted Black girls. *Gifted Child Today*, 43(2), 86–100.

Anderson, B. N., & Martin, J. A. (2018). The survival of the gifted Black girls: What K–12 educators need to know about teaching gifted Black girls battling perfectionism and stereotype threat. *Gifted Child Today*, 41(3), 117–124.

Boylorn, R. M. (2016). On being at home with myself: Blackgirl autoethnography as research praxis. *International Review of Qualitative Research*, 9(1), 44–58.

Chavous, T., & Cogburn, C. D. (2007). Superinvisible women: Black girls and women in education. *Black Women, Gender & Families*, 1(2), 24–51.

Collins, P. H. (1986, 2003). Learning from the outsider within: The sociological significance of Black feminist thought. *Social problems*, 33(6), s14–s32.

Crenshaw, K. (1991). Race, gender, and sexual harassment. *Southern California Law Review*, 65, 1467.

Davis, D. J., Reynolds, R., & Jones, T. B. (2011). Promoting the inclusion of tenure earning Black women in academe: Lessons for leaders in education. *Florida Journal of Educational Administration & Policy*, 5(1), 28–41.

Dillard, C. B. (2012). *Learning to (Re)member the things we've learned to forget: Endarkened feminisms, spirituality, and the sacred nature of research and teaching. Black studies and critical thinking* (Vol. 18). Peter Lang.

Esnard, T., & Cobb-Roberts, D. (2018). *Black women, academe, and the tenure process in the United States and the Caribbean*. Springer.

Evans, S. Y. (2007). Women of color in American higher education. *Thought & Action*, 23, 131–138.

Evans-Winters, V. E., & Love, B. L. (Eds.). (2015). *Black feminism in education: Black women speak back, up, and out*. Peter Lang Incorporated, International Academic Publishers.

Franklin, A. J. (1999). Invisibility syndrome and racial identity development in psychotherapy and counseling African American men. *The Counseling Psychologist*, 27(6), 761–793.

Gholson, M. L. (2016). Clean corners and algebra: A critical examination of the constructed invisibility of black girls and women in mathematics. *Journal of Negro Education*, 85(3), 290–301.

Griffin, K. A., Bennett, J. C., & Harris, J. (2013). Marginalizing merit?: Gender differences in Black faculty D/discourses on tenure, advancement, and professional success. *The Review of Higher Education*, 36(4), 489–512.

Haynes, C., Stewart, S., & Allen, E. (2016). Three paths, one struggle: Black women and girls battling invisibility in US classrooms. *The Journal of Negro Education*, 85(3), 380–391.

hooks, b. (1984). *Feminist theory: From center to margin*. South End Press.

Hughes, R. L., & Howard-Hamilton, M. F. (2003). Insights: Emphasizing issues that affect African American women. *New directions for student services*, 2003(104), 95–104.

Jordan, J. (2007). *Directed by desire: The collected poems of June Jordan*. Copper Canyon Press.

National Center for Education Statistics (NCES) home page, part of the U.S. Department of Education. (2017). Retrieved October 13, 2022, from https://nces.ed.gov/

Patton, L. D., Crenshaw, K., Haynes, C., & Watson, T. N. (2016). Why we can't wait: (Re) examining the opportunities and challenges for Black women and girls in education (guest editorial). *The Journal of Negro Education, 85*(3), 194–198.

Pittman, C. T. (2010). Race and gender oppression in the classroom: The experiences of women faculty of color with white male students. *Teaching Sociology, 38*(3), 183–196.

1
NAVIGATING THE DOCTORAL EXPERIENCE AS FIRST-GENERATION, GIFTED BLACK WOMEN

Our Path, Our Voice

Brittany N. Anderson and Shaquinta L. Richardson

Brittany: I don't think we understood the type of experience we were having. I don't think we understood how often you'd be surrounded by all of this brilliance. We support each other, we're here for each other, we're not pitting each other against the other. It was never a competition.
Shaquinta: Like flames—I see her light, my light can be like that too. It doesn't have to look the same way, but I have the ability for my light to shine just as bright, and I love looking at her light.

Historically, Black women and girls have been deliberately excluded from educational spaces, and with this exclusion, talent identification, career pathways, pipelines, and advancement have been out of reach for many. Although educational advancements have been made in support of Black women and girls, much work remains to be done. As a means to promote pathways to change, Black feminist scholars have advocated for the inclusion of Black women and girls' experiences in a way that addresses the complex intersectionality of their cultural knowings (Wing, 1997). These "knowings" help us to not only think critically about sound solutions, but to also honor and amplify the voices that were once silenced so that their needs are incorporated into a more equitable and just narrative. The unique needs of Black women and girls can be further understood and supported through an endarkened epistemological lens, one that also addresses problems related to the oppressed experiences of Black women (Dillard, 2012).

DOI: 10.4324/9781003292180-2

A central focus of this chapter and text situates the ways formally identified/high-ability gifted Black women, as a collective, created and later disrupted common narratives associated with navigating doctoral programs at a Predominately White Institution (PWI), *Southeastern University*. To define giftedness/high-ability, we use the definition outlined by the federal Elementary and Secondary Education Act (2015) as

> Students, children, or youth who give evidence of high achievement capability in areas such as intellectual, creative, artistic, or leadership capacity, or in specific academic fields, and who need services and activities not ordinarily provided by the school in order to fully develop those capabilities.
>
> *(Title IX, Part A, Definition 22)*

This collective, informally known as the Sista Scholars, organically formed around our intersecting identities, namely race and gender, interests, graduate organizations, and program proximity. Our collective uniquely formed synergistic academic and social spaces that actively centered liberation, joy, healing, academic and mental health accountability, and community engagement.

We position this work by framing our experiences as first-generation doctoral students, situating *homeplace* as under-resourced, rural- and urban-characteristic areas of the South (Boylorn, 2016). To explore our endarkened epistemology, we focused attention on our congruent experiences as gifted-identified Black girls/women, anchoring our P–16 and graduate work. As we examined these narratives through memory work and duoethnography, we nuanced family socialization and schooling, and the translation of said experiences in our doctoral programs through a gifted lens.

Conceptual Framework and Methodology

To ground the scholarship of understanding our lived experiences, we lean on Boylorn's (2016) work on critical autoethnography. Boylorn (2016) shared in her journey:

> I have been trying to get at home with myself for as long as I can remember. Comfortable in my skin, proud of where I come from, easy with the ways/s I am when I navigate back and forth from homes, back and forth in the South, back and forth from myself.
>
> *(p. 45)*

As we unpacked being at home with ourselves, we actively questioned who we were in the context of place, and how nuancing the homeplace can create space for vulnerability, resistance, and surrender, and later career pathways in our doctoral programs (hooks, 1990; Boylorn, 2016). We use an endarkened lens to situate our intersectional experiences navigating our K–12, undergraduate, and doctoral programs as gifted, first-generation scholars. Endarkened epistemology, coupled with personal reflexivity, was foregrounded to immerse ourselves in the memory work of our lived experiences, through multivocal and multisituational standpoints and representations (Boylorn, 2016; Adams & Holman Jones, 2011). Rather than presenting our narratives as fragmented, truncated ways of knowing, we situate our Blackgirl [one word] duoethnographies as both/and, composite, multifaceted experiences (Boylorn, 2016). Blackgirl [one word] "rejects compartmentalizing Blackgirls' lives, stories, and bodies and serves as a symbolic transgression to see them/us as complex and whole" (Hill, 2019, p. 3). We especially felt the need to amplify Blackgirl narratives through an intersectional lens in gifted education scholarship, considering that our narratives are often framed in a static, fractured, single social category, consequently creating a one-dimensional perspective. This limited perspective reduces the fullness of our experiences, and we aimed to shatter the ceilings and raise the floors.

Design and Analyses

Using qualitative methods to explore our narratives, we utilized duoethnographies to share our critical ethnographic accounts, detailing our experiences through paired and individual voice and prose, operating in both formal and informal language of our choosing. According to Sawyer and Norris (2013), duoethnography is a collaborative research methodology in which two or more researchers engage in a dialogue on their disparate histories, in a given phenomenon. We frame and position our intersectional experiences of knowing, learning, and doing as Black women, at the center of this work (Dillard, 2012; Evans-Winters, 2015). To understand our particular, but shared experiences, we interviewed each other using the same questions. As we co-constructed our Blackgirl duoethnographical renderings through personal reflexivity, memory work (Boylorn, 2016), and open-coding, we identified similar themes across family socialization, gender identity, and gifted-identified status. Through this memory-work and reflexivity, we used what Boylorn (2016) discusses as ethnographic reflexivity, cogitating on ways that our lived experiences influence our research and practice; troubling the ways these gifted identification labels impacted our K–12 schooling and beyond. When using gifted-identified, we mean formal identification for gifted and advanced programming in K–12 and participation in enrichment opportunities and Honors/Dual-Enrollment/ Advanced Placement courses.

In this chapter, we discuss how our low-income backgrounds, first-generation college status, and gifted identities shaped many of our educational experiences, and were cornerstones to us navigating our doctoral studies. We include how our gendered socialization, understanding of friendship with other women, and familial experiences interplay with our educational experiences. We continue by including ways in which leaning on our tribe of Black women empowered us, helped us navigate the difficulties in predominantly white settings, and created a supportive community of accountability. Lastly, we include recommendations and affirmations for other Black women exploring or currently enrolled in doctoral programs.

Redefining Self through Community: Shaquinta's Story

Family Socialization

I grew up in a family of Black women. There were a few men on the periphery, but the women were at the forefront of my upbringing. The women in my family line were often domestic or field workers who endured abuse out in the world, as well as at home. Still, I heard many stories of their resistance to the structures (and often the men) who oppressed them. My grandmother was 4'11" standing at her tallest. My grandfather was 6'5", yet I knew from a very young age that she would not back down from him. My mother was a single mother most of my life with the support of my grandmother. When my older sister was old enough to work at 14, she also supported us. My father grew up in New York after his parents migrated there from South Carolina (SC). He moved back to SC as a teenager, where he struggled to adjust to Southern culture (read: racism). He was in prison for much of my childhood, and while he was often absent, he always made sure I knew I was his pride and joy.

With limited resources and unsteady housing conditions, I had moved approximately 16 times before the age of 18. My mother worked in various plants and fast food restaurants, sometimes at the same time to take care of us. My childhood was like that of many Black families; "scratchin and survivin," but also full of support. Because of my upbringing, there were several cultural messages around gender identity, academic success, and respectability that have influenced my educational journey. Some of those experiences are outlined as we position this book.

Gender Identity. During our duoethnographic interviews, one memory in particular stood out regarding my identity as a young girl where I stated:

> I remember messages about being fast. That's one thing about me specifically. I remember getting a whooping from my granny with a wet rag when I was 8 for being fast...There was a girl who lived across the street from me who had a pool. My mom bought me a two-piece swimsuit, so I had a two-piece. I went over there to swim, I came back, and I don't remember what I was doing, but she said I was being fast and I got a whooping with a wet rag for being fast.

That particular whooping stood out as a core memory and one of the worst whoopings I had received (even though I got A LOT of them for being "hard-headed"). From my Granny's perspective, I was posturing like an adult, with my hand on my hip, with no cover up and for that, I deserved to be punished. *At the age of 8.* From that very young age, there was a general labeling of me as a "fast-tail girl." I was taught to believe early that it was my responsibility, even as a child, to carry myself a certain way to be seen as acting appropriately and to prevent being punished. I repeatedly received messages about not getting pregnant or focusing on school instead of those "nappy-headed boys." It did not matter that I was a gifted student. The message was to simply stop being "fast," so I do not get pregnant and end up like another one of "those girls" and ruin my life forever.

There was a lot of messaging around who I should *not be* and what I should *not do*, as a young girl in preparation for becoming a woman. Most of the messaging shamed sexuality and positioned women as tools for the use of others, particularly men. However, my mother also preached to always be independent and never depend on a man. I understand now, the lessons that were bestowed upon me were the lessons my mother had learned from her mother (Granny) based on lessons from her mother (Grandma Lillie) and her mothers before her, with some variation based on their own lived experiences. This was the transgenerational transmission of stifling womanhood; consistently being told what not to do to prevent being a target of men or white people. While I have a different understanding of these lessons as an adult—which were adaptive at the time for them—the lessons of how to be a woman in this world were missing and were ultimately what created challenges for me throughout my journey and growth through adulthood. This contributed to why being surrounded by so many other Black women was paramount to my growth during my doctoral journey. These connections helped me to explore and redefine my own womanhood from a more critical space. This is a prime example of how multiple influences interact in our lives. In addition to my family's teachings, like many of my formative experiences, my identity was also shaped by my academic experiences. My academic journey added another layer to the intersection of being Black and a woman.

Academic Expectations. While the importance of education was always emphasized, no one in my immediate or close extended family had a college degree, and few had a high school diploma. I was an early reader and was quickly identified as gifted in my elementary school. I was advanced in all the subjects and was headstrong. My father tells the story of me tying my shoe at a fairly young age and realizing that I was determined to figure it out on my own when I screamed "No!" when he tried to help. They knew I wanted to be a doctor when I grew up so my father would send me self-illustrated cards from prison with a picture of a young woman with a white coat and stethoscope encouraging me to keep working hard in school. My mother would not accept a grade lower than a B, but I wanted A's. I was always determined to be the best in school. What I didn't understand at the time was how difficult it would be to be perceived that way. Like many Black people, I heard, "you have to be twice as good to get half as far." I learned early on that Black people were seen as less intelligent, and I knew I was not. My father preached to me about the way his teachers treated him differently in school because of his cultural differences (he moved from New York) and how that was the reason he did not graduate. My father is brilliant. But he was painted as a problem kid from the moment he entered school in the South. Both my parents knew of the challenges that were ahead. Those messages would start to actualize for me as I continued my educational journey.

Schooling Experiences

K–12. I attended multiple elementary schools, but I had similar experiences across the schools. I was often the only Black person in my gifted classes, so I stood out. In second grade, my gifted and talented program teacher told my mother that, "gifted children will try you so you have to watch them." My mother took that to heart. She would second-guess what I would tell her because she constantly worried that I was trying to outsmart her. It created a dynamic where I would have to prove that I was not lying or trying to outsmart her, and she would heavily scrutinize the most minute actions. I would be punished for things I did not do, which led me to resent my mother and distrust my teachers because I felt they would use my intelligence against me. I subconsciously learned that my giftedness could be used as a weapon against me by white women to "keep me in my place," which I would not have been able to articulate then, but understand now. I couldn't help but think, no one tells white parents to watch their little girls because they're too smart.

Simultaneously, I was being told by my peers that I was not good enough because of my race. During the interview, I highlighted a defining moment during middle school:

> I had a moment with one of my white peers…I think we were joking about something and I considered her a friend. I thought she was. And I cannot remember the conversation fully but we were joking about something and I might have said, "I'm better at [this]." I can't remember, I was a little smart ass. But she said, "Oh, no Black person will ever be better than me." And that sticks with me. That has stuck with me throughout my entire life. I will never forget. I remember what she was wearing. I remember those words…That was a defining moment in my life.

That moment stuck with me throughout my school career. I internalized that message. Whether I believed I was smarter or better at school, it would not matter because they would still think that I could not possibly be as good, much less, better academically and the teachers would make sure I did not "get too big for my britches." Because I defined myself by how good I was academically and experienced so much pressure from my family to excel while also having other parts of me degraded and minimized, it created much anxiety and internal crises when it came to interacting in the classroom and pursuing higher education. I was tasked with being exceptional for my family while knowing I was both too much and not enough in academic spaces.

Undergraduate. Like many other Black people who go to Historically Black Colleges and Universities (HBCUs), my HBCU was the first time I was surrounded by students and faculty who primarily looked like me and seemingly came from similar backgrounds. It was the first time I truly saw the diversity of brilliance that is Black people. It was also the first time that I was exposed to more affluent Black families. It was the first time that I was not the "smart Black girl" because there were lots of smart Black women and men surrounding me. While this was a beautiful position to be in, it also created somewhat of an identity crisis because, if I am no longer the "smart Black girl," then who am I?

Having the space to explore that question was truly one of the greatest gifts of my HBCU experience. I did not have to stand out for this *one* thing. I did not have to stand out at all, and if I did, it would be for something extraordinary. I previously thought simply being smart was extraordinary, which is problematic at best and anti-Black at worst. Because everyone was smart, I had to develop my other gifts and multiple aspects of my personality. I met professors and peers that nurtured those gifts without making me feel special or different in ways that diminished my personhood. The "smart Black girl" became the student who is good at math with strong reasoning and critical thinking skills, good at helping other students learn how to navigate certain skills, funny to some, not so funny to others, a dope stepper, sweet and kind, but quiet, among other things. People saw past the shock of me being "smart" because I am Black and saw more.

In addition to the educational component of my experience at an HBCU, there was also a cultural fortitude that was added to my experience. I learned things about the history of Black people in this country and beyond, from a strength- and resilience-based perspective, that I would not have gotten at a predominantly white institution without majoring in African American Studies. I was able to see Black people from different backgrounds being and learning together. I also witnessed how strong our cultural values are as a people. Kenya from Connecticut had some of the same familial experiences and could relate to cultural traditions without having ever crossed paths previously. There is such comfort in knowing that the space you are in is understanding and supportive of who you are as a human being rather than only a racialized body in their institution, hence why this book was created. Being in a place where you do not have to make safe spaces based on your race because the institution itself is a safe space makes a huge difference in our comfort and ability to perform. Not having to create bonds out of necessity for survival, but primarily out of shared interest deepens our humanity. Had I not had that experience, I do not know that I would have had the academic or personal fortitude to withstand the graduate school process.

Graduate Programs. During my graduate programs, I shifted back into being one of the few Black women in my educational spaces. However, this time around I was much more grounded in myself to take on the task of managing these experiences as a Black woman pursuing doctoral education. While Black women have the most degrees statistically (Esnard & Cobb-Roberts, 2018; NCES, 2017), we are still the minority within the academy. Within my own field of therapy, Black therapists make up 2–4 percent of the field (Mental Health America, 2022). My department was separated by specialization, and within my specialization was one other Black woman who was two years ahead of me. Of my cohort of seven, I was the only BIPOC person. One of my biggest challenges was sitting in rooms with other budding scholars and established researchers in the field, hearing information that was either based on or perpetuated stereotypes about Black people, but not having the "data" to back up my disagreement. I could clearly see where the bias was in the work or the gaps in the research but did not have the weight to my voice that comes with years of doing research. In addition, I had to listen to other students' microaggressions daily.

Back home, life continued moving, with family members and friends getting married, having children, starting businesses, and experiencing a life that looked entirely different from my daily reality as a graduate student. I received the dreaded, "how much longer do you have in school?" question every time I went home. I was not excused from the questions regarding marriage and children and the insinuation that I would be old and lonely with my degrees. While there were people who were proud of me for sure, my family did not have the context to understand why I kept going to school and how difficult the experience was for me because I was "always so smart." When I decided to start the doctoral journey, an acquaintance even asked me what I was running from. He could not understand why I wanted to continue going to school rather than working in my hometown, settling down, and following the typical married-with-kids path. Or really just kids, if I'm honest.

The experience was isolating at times because not only did I feel out of place amongst my peers, I was also struggling significantly in personal life. In addition to navigating the expectations of friends and family, I also experienced some of the most difficult times of my life financially. One of the challenges of being a first generation college graduate was the lack of context and understanding of what I was truly getting myself into. As much as I planned and budgeted, I found myself almost destitute during my first semester because of the unknown costs associated with the journey (conferences, extra fees, delayed funding, etc.). Because my family already had limited resources, I was not able to turn to them for assistance.

There already is not much information on the doctoral journey as is. The lack of information is exacerbated by the limited exposure first-generation students have to the world of academia as a whole and what it entails beyond academic rigor. Departmental, institutional, and funding politics all played into the success of completing the program. The first year is when professors start to parse out who they see potential in and are willing to work with on research and committee chairing. I struggled terribly that first year and feared I would not have the support I needed to make it through.

My saving grace during my doctoral journey was the network of other Black students, particularly the Black women in my department—which I was lucky to have several—and the women in the graduate student organization for marginalized students. This unusually large network of Black women was a source of comfort during challenging times, sounding boards for how to navigate difficult situations, writing partners when we needed to get things done, and fellow shit-talkers when we needed to let it all out. They helped me strategize, fed me, gave me rides when needed, and provided comfort when I allowed feelings of failure to creep in. These women showed me how to navigate department politics and kept me going when I wanted to give up. They also normalized that very real desire on a continual basis, but we did not allow each other to give in because while our departments may not have valued our work, we reminded each other why each one of us was needed.

Our university—to no credit of their own—had a resource that many other universities do not have, and that resource was the connection to other Black women/people. In the words of one of our contributors, Dr. Joan Collier, "We didn't survive because of them [the University]. We survived in spite of them." We survived and thrived because we had each others' backs. The idea for this book was developed based on our experiences with these women. We are honored to have their stories heard.

Despise not Humble Beginnings: Situating Place, Gender, Class, and Giftedness: Brittany's Story

Family Socialization

"Despise not humble beginnings" is a phrase my Mama has frequently used to contextualize our past, current, and future trajectories. In defining the gifts of the present, she knew not to forget the past, and anchored historical events in our daily lives. Post emancipation, both my maternal and paternal family members settled into neighboring rural areas in the South, working primarily in domestics, food service, and agriculture. To contextualize place, the majority of my extended family lived in close proximity to the plantations where they were once enslaved. As a result of labor exploitation, racism, lack of educational resources/opportunities, and low pay, my family members grappled with generational poverty. As a geographical area, community members primarily subsidized their incomes with government funding and other sources, and often worked in domestic roles/labor. The community has been, and continues to be, a segregated area, with vast inequities in terms of educational opportunities and access to jobs with a living wage. In addition, this area also has a historical legacy of lynching and terrorizing communities of color. For context, this area did not fully integrate schools until the 1970s, and racial tensions are still an issue for many people of color there.

Despite the regional oppression, my family has always utilized our collective village (extended family and friends) to ensure that my care and academic needs were met. My mother functioned as a single mother, and in my earlier years we experienced a great deal of transiency. As a note, the bordering towns are smaller and streamlined, and though transient in terms of address, I still attended the same schools. During times of housing instability, my great-grandparents served as caretakers, in addition to being after-school and summer care. My mother, grandmothers, and paternal great-grandparents served as bedrocks in terms of my familial socialization and are included in my analysis. With different generational worldviews and perspectives, a conduit of my endarkened perspective centered around gender identity and academic expectations, similar to Shaquinta's narrative.

Gender Identity. In terms of my gender identity development, there were traditional conversations about how women and girls conduct themselves, particularly in the phases of girlhood. There were also clear parameters established by the family matriarchs about a "child's place," and ways they expected me to operate within these boundaries. Presently, I still ponder the ways this shows up in my current practice of navigating family dynamics. As I reflect on my development as a young girl, there were several "protective" factors many of the elders and family members in the community engaged in that can now be viewed as gender shaming; but, from their perspective, they were protecting your innocence. Maintaining and sheltering young girls from the perverse nature of men was incredibly important to those in my community. As a caveat to my upbringing, the elders and other family members focused on young girls not being considered "fast" and similarly, having been dubbed as the "smart kid" there were often conversations framed around respectability that I now frame as "people pleasing." From their assessment, young girls acted in ways that did not posture or emulate that of a grown woman. You were encouraged to be seen and not heard, and often speaking your "mind" was also considered disrespectful. Holding several thoughts at once, I contended with the tightrope of these fragile boundaries because causing disruption was not something I wanted to do. As a young child, I was rather observant and wanted to assuage any additional challenges my mother was already facing, aiming to not be a burden in any way. This in turn created a pattern, minimizing any foreseen obstacle, grounding my actions around what will be good for others (i.e. people pleasing).

In addition to the general dynamics of an impoverished rural community, without access to a platitude of opportunities and exposure, gender socialization was heavily influenced by Southern rituals and traditional indoctrination(s) and teachings of the Christian church. Women and girls dressed modestly, operated in a domesticated capacity—were caretakers of families and men— and worked diligently without seeking gratitude. Growing up in a Southern, Primitive Baptist tradition, men are typically viewed as leaders in the decision-making processes and operations. However, in my community, many of the "mothers" in the church handled these operations, my great-grandmother being one. Her role as the "mother matriarch" in church and the community, taught me about leadership, positionality, persuasion (even within the bounds of patriarchy), effective communication (delivery), and diplomacy. In this community, women typically received more education than men, and used this information to advise as much as they could. The women started businesses and sustained outreach, engagement, and wellness in the community. The focus on serving the community and serving God was a cornerstone for my mother and all my grandmothers, and they, in turn, instilled these principles in me. These practices are grounded in my present work, pedagogical practices, and views on community engagement.

As I think about my evolving identity as a Southern Black woman, I have developed and reshaped some views from the traditional approaches of my upbringing. Having others in our sister circle from rural, low-income areas, with a first-generation status has been instrumental in this exploration and self-discovery of how I situate and understand my identity as a gifted Black woman.

Academic Expectations. My mother played an instrumental role in making sure literacy and reading achievement was foundational to my academic success. Receiving stellar grades was a spoken and unspoken expectation in my household. As the oldest child in my family, birth order played a significant role in the messaging, and how my success and efforts were viewed. I was always considered an intelligent child by those in my community, and my family expected nothing but success from me. However, upon reflection, operationally defining how success materialized was not something we truly captured. Therefore, I took success to mean high grades because that was often the marker, and always doing well, established a perfectionistic, people-pleasing personality (this would not serve me well later). Achievement and success for me were framed by stellar grades, awards, reading achievement, and promotion; engaging in critical thinking, resistance, and pushing bounds were not considered products of intellect because children, especially girls, should remain in their "place."

The discourse around my gifted identity was not something we explicitly discussed in my home, but many of my talents were identified and developed at home first. My mother was influential in cultivating my academic prowess—pushing me to do my best, decreasing distractions in our home, and focusing on literacy and my interests. Despite the fluctuations in our homebase, there was always a sense of structure, focus on accountability, and set responsibilities, even as a young child. These early practices established by my mother, grandmothers, and great-grandparents were instrumental in my development as a gifted student. Her busy schedule, and status as a single mother, with relatively limited insider knowledge of navigating school structures, did not mitigate my mother's focus on my academic abilities in our home. Although I performed well at school, much of my learning and talent development occurred within informal learning spaces: home, community spaces, church, and summer camps. My first way of understanding multimodal learning, particularly experiential learning, happened in my grandmother's kitchen. Much of how I situate learning, teaching, and doing is through an experiential lens, which I attribute to my upbringing.

Schooling Experiences

K–12. My formative schooling experience (Pre-K–5) consisted of attending Head Start, primary, and elementary school in a small town in the southwest, with a population of 4,000 individuals. Because of the smaller population, the number of schools was limited: one primary, elementary, intermediate, middle, and high school. To contextualize the demographic and economic make-up of the town, approximately 60 percent of the residents are white, 20 percent African American, and 20 percent Hispanic/Latinx. In 2016, the percentage of residents living in poverty was 33.1 percent. In 2000, the median income was $24,880, and in 2016 was $41,814. In 2018, of those attending this district's schools, 56.5 percent of students were considered at-risk of dropping out of school, and only 1.8 percent of students qualified for gifted and talented programming and services. These statistics are important to note because there were pervasive inequitable practices in these schools for children of color. Rarely were students of color referred for gifted services, and my own experiences of being from one of "those families," colored some of the interactions I had with teachers in these spaces. I did have a few teachers that recognized my ability early on, but I was repeatedly denied for gifted placement; at the time, there were not any students of color selected for the program. Each time there was the explanation that I did not perform well on a "moving target," although my grades and academic assessments were exemplary. During my K–5 educational experiences, I had several racially charged incidents with teachers, specifically during fourth grade. It was always this position of "putting me in my place." However, my mother took charge, and handled these situations accordingly.

Transitioning to middle school, we moved from this rural town to an urban-characteristic (Milner, 2012) area with a population of 271,000 individuals, located centrally in the state. With this change, I was immediately placed in gifted services and classes. Also, with this transition, there was a demographic shift—a majority of African Americans and Hispanic/Latinx populations—compared to the predominately white schools I had attended before. Most of the schools in this district were Title I/low-income. The economic demographic was similar; most occupants of the city were considered low-income and battled with poverty, failing schools, and not having access to jobs paying a living wage. I attended a low-performing school, but several teachers, specifically Black teachers, were invested in making sure I did well, offering opportunities that came across their desks, and encouraging me to push forward, despite our school lacking curricular resources. However, there were pervasive attitudes from my peers that academic excelling was deemed as "acting white." Here, I mostly focused on getting exemplary grades, but rarely was my intellectual curiosity engaged. In 7th grade, I had an opportunity to attend a summer enrichment camp for low-income gifted students, and from that experience, I am still reaping the benefits. There, I extended the scope of my love of learning; there, I received exposure to subjects and content that were not offered at my school, and it was there that I began grappling with my gifted identity as a Black girl, and how to navigate these multiple identities and marginalization.

I continued to high school with a narrow view of success, mainly academic achievement and stellar grades. This did work out well for me in a sense, I graduated from a National Academy Foundation program as class Valedictorian, and received numerous scholarships to attend a private, esteemed institution of higher education. However, I did not attend to the social interactions with my peers, racial identity development, social-emotional development, and my continued battles with perfectionism.

Undergraduate. I attended a private, parochial, PWI for undergrad, and this transition proved to be challenging for me. I pivoted once again to being one of the few persons of color in my courses, and now with a true understanding of what my economic, first-generation status meant. Yes, I was intelligent, but often did not feel this way in my courses. I contended with professors not believing I was capable or undermining my potential because of perceived behavioral interactions and engagement. I also contended with classmates that frequently engaged in and extrapolated culturally and academically deficit views and narratives about my experiences based on the schools I attended, and the area I lived in. I was fatigued on multiple levels: "fighting" for my professors to see that I belonged, fighting negative stereotypes about Black women and people of color in a majority white and middle to upper-middle class institution, gifted attributes/identity, peer-group belonging/alignment, and racial identity. I did not know then, but these were not my battles to fight. Despite the challenges, I found my passion for working in early education, and continued to cultivate my talents in elementary school settings as a classroom teacher. There, I found my love of working with creativity, engaging the youth in critical thinking and discourse, and watching my students move beyond boundaries that may have been placed on them.

Graduate Experience. We shared our Blackgirl K–12 narratives because of the recursive nature of our Blackgirl experiences, and how it "followed" us into our graduate programs. Things that we had unearthed in our K–12 and undergraduate experiences continued to be placeholders in our understanding of self, perceived understanding of belonging, and academic expectations and engagement. In my master's and doctoral program, I continued to be one of the few Black women in my courses and programming. I was blessed to have an advisor of color that shaped and invested in my matriculation through the program. Although this individual had a personal investment in my success, this investment could not protect me from the wiles of gendered racism—through the microaggressions and invisibility I experienced in classes, to interactions with peers and professors. I personally contended with imposter syndrome, maladaptive perfectionism, stereotype threat, and constantly trying to prove I belonged in this space. Moving beyond these contentions I felt in these spaces with professors, peers, and other scholars, I found my voice in experiences. My background, schooling experience, and representation as a member of several underrepresented groups was my voice- a lived, authentic experience as a student and classroom teacher, that many of my peers had only read about. I had experienced these issues in our textbooks and articles in real-time.

Much of the scholarship seemingly created this dichotomy of what "research" should be, and the methods that should accompany it to be considered a scholar. However, I was finding ways in our university-school-community engagement that there was more than the "traditional" pathways to be considered a scholar; although I was being guided towards these traditional routes. This moment of insight gave me the push I needed to showcase my brilliance, rather than hiding in the corner because I was not familiar with terminology, or my academic writing was not on par with expectations. My practical, lived experience gave me entry into spaces not previously explored, connecting with students and educators in ways that bridged theory and practice, and served the community.

Endarkening Gifted Blackgirlhood Narratives. Once I moved beyond the frayed understanding that my experience was an asset rather than a liability, I was able to tap into my true capabilities, with my sister circle supporting me, exalting my greatness, and listening to me vent when things were going array. I observed ways where our pathways were converging, despite our varying backgrounds, anchoring themes around perfectionism, ways that places and spaces exacerbated our anxieties, and the unhealthy and sometimes defective methods our knowledge was demented in the name of academic excellence. They were there with me to serve the community, engage in discussions about racial identity, have discourse about Black womanhood, and ways for mitigating imposter syndrome. In this space, many of us had a shared faith, and several of our interactions were grounded in our spiritual beliefs. We prayed together, carpooled to church, had Sunday dinners, and one sister scholar in particular (Dr. Martin) would lead us in song. "Til we meet again" will always be a song in my heart. We were guided by our purpose, and in that purpose found ways to grapple with the scholarship. I began uncovering ways to be at home with myself (Boylorn, 2016), anchoring the wholeness of myself, my experiences, and ventured to co-create liberated views of gifted Black women and girls.

This sister circle protected me from feeling isolated, strategized with me, offered social outlets, created writing groups and spaces, grieved with me during family death, and assisted me with coursework when needed. I also reciprocated these practices with them, creating mutually beneficial practices that were grounded in our collective. These safe spaces proved to be a sanctuary for me when I felt discouraged or less than—a true space of belonging. They knew of my experiences because they too were navigating similar experiences. Not only were these spaces helpful socially and academically, but they also helped with narrowing a research area/agenda. In this space, I begin to frame ways of knowing and being through the lens of gifted Black girls and women, creating questions of inquiry, disrupting false narratives, and establishing spaces for memory work. I found that many of my sister scholars had been gifted-identified and were experiencing issues with perfectionism and other social-emotional issues. This realization created a niche research area for me, considering very few scholars had explored gifted Black girls and women's experiences in schools and doctoral programs. It was here that I began to fully understand that for me to create a pathway that honors this memory work, experiences in the classroom, familial heritage, and cultural traditions. I could disrupt the notions of invisibility in the scholarship with other Black girls and women. With this scholarship and research, I could disrupt the elusive fortification of what gifted education has been for Black girls and women. It was here that I understood that the path I was following through the traditional navigation of the academy was not my own, and surmised what I would need to do within myself to quiet the voices of "people-pleasing" and perfectionism to chart different ways of knowing and doing in gifted, Black Girlhood, and urban education research.

Converging Narratives

Through our duoethnographic process, we noticed several converging themes that shaped our individual experiences. As first-generation scholars, this journey was about coming into an understanding of self, BEYOND this gifted identity that we held so dearly. These experiences demonstrated the commonalities regarding family and gender socialization, giftedness, and gendered racism in our educational journeys. Lastly, we explored the ways we were socialized to experience friendships and community with other women. We have outlined these commonalities below in preparation for discussion on how we navigated the doctoral journey, influenced by our individual journeys, leading us both to the women who contributed to this work.

Sexuality and Shaming

One of the most prominent themes within both interviews was the idea of not being "fast" as a young girl, and the prevention narratives of being another teenage pregnancy statistic. This was outlined in Shaquinta's narrative with her grandmother, and Brittany's narrative with modesty in the church. Gender shaming is prevalent within the Black community, as women and girls are taught to be "modest" and not tempt men (Fitch & Nazaretian, 2019). We also saw this in the consistent cautions to avoid pregnancy at all costs, as this was the ultimate shame and derailing of our academic success. Whether through religious doctrine, fear-mongering, or old-fashioned shaming and degrading, being a woman meant constant policing of our behaviors, words, and interactions with boys and men. Again, these messages were not from a malicious place, but cornerstones of tradition.

Perspectives on Women Navigating Relationships with Women

Despite our clear position around creating spaces with other Black women as a best-practice for navigating doctoral programs, this was not part of our familial socialization. This notion emerged through our conversations around family socialization, and how we were taught that platonic relationships with other women were challenging and to be avoided.

Whether explicitly through conversation or implicitly through action or lack thereof, we were both taught that platonic relationships with women, specifically healthy relationships/friendships, were nearly impossible to navigate and were to be avoided—"women can't be trusted" or "women are messy." Because of this socialization, we both found it difficult to conceptualize how to be in close, healthy relationships with other women. However, we both knew this was something we needed and really yearned for during our journeys. As stated by Brittany:

> The Black women that I met here, well there at [school], were just my bedrock. This was the first time that I felt like I formed true relationships with Black women, collectively, like where we're not one here and one here. I learned a lot about myself, my identity, and how I wanted to make my way in the world.

Being connected to so many dynamic women, all of whom were here to support one another was such an unfamiliar experience that also felt so much like home. As we narrated our personal experiences with this issue, we found that we were often learning and unlearning social conditioning around friendships with other Black women. We asserted that although these were "truths" or lived experiences with those in our family, we would not let that deter us from finding joy, support, and accountability in these spaces. We also discussed how we shared similar aspirations to create spaces for other Black women in our personal and professional lives.

Gifted Identity

We also shared similar experiences around being gifted Black girls in our educational experiences. We shared encounters about how our white peers "dumbed" down our capabilities and intellectual ability, but at different times having to juxtapose our aptitude with our Black identities. Brittany was often shamed for being smart in her community, and the position of her academic capacity as a proximity to whiteness, often framed in gifted education literature as the "acting white phenomenon" (Ogbu, 1988). In contrast, Shaquinta was empowered by her academic capabilities, all the while also understanding that sometimes her academic candor was not always viewed in a positive light:

> I was a know it all...that was very annoying to people...So, if anything, they wanted me to stop that [correcting] for sure, for sure. But yeah. I never felt like they weren't proud of me or wanted me to stop being so smart.

We understood our status and self-identity around our intellectual prowess as "smart Black girls" and what was expected of us. As a result, the fear of failure often weighed heavily in our decision-making about career pursuits, coursework, and risk-taking. Similarly, we both noted our struggles with perfectionism and its maladaptive effects. Throughout our educational experiences, we often negotiated and grappled with our desires to be without flaw, which was perpetuated by our fear of failure and stereotype threat (Anderson & Martin, 2018; Anderson, 2020). For Shaquinta, experiences of stereotype threat and battling imposter syndrome as it related to race were not as cumbersome during her undergraduate experience, due to her attending an HBCU. However, for Brittany, her anxiety and pushing against the narrative of "not belonging" increased her maladaptive coping strategies and unhealthy associations with perfectionism. Lastly, our mothers heavily influenced our drive for success, and their efforts pushed us to pursue our goals, even if our aspirations were outside of their knowledge-base. They used every tool at their disposal to ensure we had the right opportunities.

Navigating the Doctoral Experience as First-Generation Student

The purpose of this book is not only to highlight the value of our experiences among other Black women during our doctoral journey, but also to provide some practical tools to help navigate the process. Our tools for navigation are centered on the impetus for developing this book: the idea of finding your community, specifically among other Black women. The ways in which the women featured in this book became connected is multi-faceted. Some of us met through an organized group, while others knew different women and connected us to each other as our network grew. Shaquinta expressed, "It was like, 'Oh this other woman's here [at the university]? We need to bring her [into the fold] and we need to make sure she gets some of this [community support] too.'" We knew our connections were valuable, but

> "I don't think we understood the type of experience we were having. I don't think we understood how often you'd be surrounded by all of this brilliance, and we support each other. We're here for each other, we're not pitting against each other. It was never a competition,"

said Brittany. Shaquinta echoed, "we leaned on each other, we used the knowledge that we had from each other like, 'Okay how did you do this?' That was the key."

Academic Support

The adage of "you don't know what you don't know" rings true for so many first-generation Black women during the doctoral process. Because this was a completely new experience for many of us, sharing new information was paramount to our success. The collective of women shared knowledge freely with one another (Combahee River Collective, 1977), which ties back to the idea that there was no competition amongst us, at least not enough that it prevented us from wanting to see another sister succeed. If one person gathered information from their department that they felt other women could benefit from, they would share. Developing a network of Black women from other departments within your university to diversify types of information and tools for success can enrich the doctoral experience tremendously.

In addition to developing a network, it is important to be willing to ask for help and support. Making it to the doctoral stage means that every woman to this point has likely been a shining star (e.g. gifted and TALENTED) in her own right, which may make it difficult to be vulnerable and operate in the position of "not knowing." However, everyone has multiple strengths and areas for growth. Allowing yourself to garner support for growth areas also opens you up to exhibit your own strengths in support of one another, making everyone a much stronger, well-rounded scholar.

Being a doctoral student means writing. Writing all the time. Writing all the things. WRITING, WRITING, WRITING. So, of course, so much of our time together was spent writing together in groups. As first-generation scholars, both of us struggled with commanding academic writing. The African American Vernacular English (AAVE) was our first language and navigating mainstream English to disseminate research and scholarship was a challenge. We held each other accountable to our goals, and shared resources, opportunities, pitfalls, and tools for success. At any given time, either of us could call on ten or more women to write with and utilize what Shaquinta likes to call the "collective writing energy." Whether with wine or coffee, venting about negative experiences, or getting straight to work, we had an avenue to make sure we had dedicated writing time on a regular basis, without feeling alone and disconnected as many graduate students have posited of their experiences (Brown & Watson, 2010). The message here is to develop a network. Reach out to people and be clear about your challenges, particularly with feelings of isolation. Develop a writing schedule and have a list of people whom you can call on at any given time to garner some collective writing energy.

Social Support

For Black women that identify as first-generation and are navigating their programs in PWI settings, it is of great importance they seek social support to battle feelings of isolation they may be experiencing in their programs. As these first-gen Black women matriculate through their programs, they may find themselves not being able to connect with family, physically and cognitively, due to family not being able to understand the process, constraints, and exhaustion they may be facing. Winkle-Wagner's (2009) ethnographic study examined the complexity of first-generation Black women's negotiation of familial relationships in a PWI; the study provided evidence that Black women described a sense of homelessness, not finding a space on the campus or fitting into their family of origin. Our families wanted to understand our navigation, but what we were experiencing was often hard to explain and frustrating at the same time because we felt misunderstood or underestimated. We often heard we should be "grateful" that we had the opportunity, rather than validating our concerns. During these exchanges, our sister circle was there to hear us lament and/or provide a re-frame or accountability, if needed.

Dating is a whole other story. An additional layer of our experiences as Black women are tied to the gendered nuances of partnership. From the time we are children, we are conditioned to act and present ourselves in certain ways in order to be deemed suitable for partnership, specifically with a man. Many of us experienced challenges with partnership, due to our academic status, ambition, and personal conflicts with societal expectations of women to be domestic partners, and as a result, subjugated by the men in our lives. These expectations were front and center during the doctoral process, even as we dated men who shared similar racialized experiences across the university. We were there for each other through relationship challenges and pitfalls and provided support for one another through heartbreaks, and day-to-day frustrations as we attempted to balance relationships with competing academic responsibilities. We also gave each other those loving side-eyes when needed. There was a limited pool of Black men in our social sphere as well, so navigating the complexities of proximity and relationships was a delicate balance, but contrary to messaging we received about relationships among women, we typically handled those situations with grace.

In addition, Black women in these programs will need to surround themselves with other Black women to counter racial battle fatigue, create recreational outlets, co-conspire, and engage in self-care. We have experienced instances where we would feel guilty about taking care of ourselves socially, mentally, physically, and spiritually, but our social support group was there to keep us accountable and remind us that we must give ourselves permission to breathe. This may mean hosting movie nights, game nights, cookouts, wine-downs, and holiday gatherings.

Conclusion

As first-generation scholars looking to impact the world and act as change agents, we must lean on our networks—by filling each other's cups. Completing this process is not only about academic aptitude, but perseverance. We can challenge the stereotypes of Black women in the academy, by leaning on our Sista Scholar network. Lastly, you are not your status. Yes, being first-generation may create some barriers as you navigate unknown paths, but do NOT let that deter your greatness. The world needs your work. In the words of Auntie Audre Lorde (1981), "I am not free while any woman is unfree, even when her shackles are very different from my own." We hope this chapter proves helpful for those who come after us, free from isolation, free from doubt, free from the status quo. Free to connect, free to do more than survive, but THRIVE.

References

Adams, T. E., & Holman Jones, S. (2011). Telling Stories: Reflexivity, Queer Theory, and Autoethnography. *Cultural Studies ↔ Critical Methodologies*, *11*(2), 108–116. https://doi.org/10.1177/1532708611401329

Anderson, B. N. (2020). "See me, see us": Understanding the intersections and continued marginalization of adolescent gifted Black girls. *Gifted Child Today*, *43*(2), 86–100.

Anderson, B. N., & Martin, J. A. (2018). The survival of the gifted Black girls: What K–12 educators need to know about teaching gifted Black girls battling perfectionism and stereotype threat. *Gifted Child Today*, *41*(3), 117–124.

Brown, L., & Watson, P. (2010). Understanding the experiences of female doctoral students. *Journal of Further and Higher Education*, *34*(3), 385–404.

Boylorn, R. M. (2016). On being at home with myself: Blackgirl autoethnography as research praxis. *International Review of Qualitative Research*, *9*(1), 44–58.

Collective, C. R. (1977). 'A Black Feminist Statement', (pp. 210–218).

Dillard, C. B. (2012). *Learning to (Re)member the things we've learned to forget: Endarkened feminisms, spirituality, and the sacred nature of research and teaching. Black studies and critical thinking* (Vol. 18). Peter Lang.

Esnard, T., & Cobb-Roberts, D. (2018). *Black women, academe, and the tenure process in the United States and the Caribbean*. Springer.

Evans-Winters, V. E., & Love, B. L. (Eds.). (2015). *Black feminism in education: Black women speak back, up, and out*. Peter Lang Incorporated, International Academic Publishers.

Fitch, C. H., & Nazaretian, Z. (2019). Examining gender differences in reintegrative shaming theory: The role of shame acknowledgment. *Crime, Law and Social Change*, *72*(5), 527–546.

hooks, bell (1990). *Yearning: Race, gender, and cultural politics.* Boston: South End Press.

Lorde, A. (1981). The uses of anger.

Milner IV, H. R. (2012). But what is urban education? *Urban Education, 47*(3), 556–561.

National Center for Education Statistics (NCES) home page, part of the U.S. Department of Education. (2017). Retrieved October 13, 2022, from https://nces.ed.gov/

Ogbu, J. U. (1988). *Black education: A cultural-ecological perspective,* In H. P. McAdoo (Ed.), *Black families* (pp. 169–184). Sage Publications, Inc..

Reinert, M., Fritze, D., & Nguyen, T. (2021). *The state of mental health in America 2022.* Mental Health America.

Sawyer, R. D., & Norris, J. (2013). *Duoethnography.* Oxford University Press.

Wing, A. K. (Ed.). (1997). *Critical race feminism: A reader.* NYU Press.

Winkle-Wagner, R. (2009). *The unchosen me: Race, gender, and identity among Black women in college.* JHU Press.

2

MISUNRE

Navigating the Doctoral Journey as an Exceptionally Gifted Black Woman

Jillian A. Martin, Ph.D.

In discussing this chapter with the book editors, a song lyric popped into my head about things being simple, but we make it hard (Hill, 1998, Track 2, Ex-Factor). Like any earworm, they are best handled by just playing the song, sometimes on repeat for good measure and riddance. So, I gave the song "Ex-Factor" a listen after the meeting. And then I felt compelled to do something I have done many times since its release on my thirteenth birthday: I listened to the entirety of *The Miseducation of Lauryn Hill* album. And within the album, I heard the vision of the editors for this volume, and the original exceptionally gifted Black woman for me: Lauryn Hill.

Whenever I am naming my top five list of the greatest emcees, I always name Lauryn Hill first. What artist is still touring and performing off their first and only – solo studio album? *The Miseducation of Lauryn Hill* was the first hip-hop album to win Album of the Year at the Grammy Awards. With one album, she set the record for most Grammy nominations and wins by a female artist. Ms. Hill, for her solo work or work with the Fugees, is present on every list of the greatest albums ever made. *Miseducation* also put concepts of diasporan music on the map sampling from African American, African, and Caribbean musical legacies (Morgan, 2018). The album is a work of art that is uniquely and distinctly Black. Even the name of the album pays homage to Black history and culture by borrowing from Woodson's (1933) *The Miseducation of the Negro*.

The album was deeply personal to me as a Black girl coming of age in the 90s and 00s. I resonated with Ms. Hill's confusion, her longing

DOI: 10.4324/9781003292180-3

to understand and be understood, her frustration with the way things were around her. I resonated with her feeling disconnected and unsure of herself. I resonated with her questioning the world around her. With time and experience, each lyric took on new and different meanings. Her music helped me to understand intersectionality theory long before I read Crenshaw (2017). It helped me to understand communication and vulnerability before I was exposed to Brown (2015). Before I read Walker (2004, 2011, 2021), Collins (2002, Lorde (1982), Angelou (1991, 1997), or Butler (2012), I heard Lauryn. She helped me to untangle my confusion and frustration with the world around me. She admitted that she was miseducated. She admitted that she did not understand the world around her. She was complex and full of contradictions.

Exceptionally and profoundly gifted children are children whose capacity to learn is significantly advanced even beyond the average for the intellectually gifted (Gross, 1999). It is important to note, however, that we are talking about academic potential, rather than school performance (Gross, 1999). I think that is why *Miseducation* was my first thought as I began to conceptualize this chapter. Ms. Hill embodies what it means to be an exceptionally gifted Black woman. She, whether unwittingly or intentionally, complicated things that everyone else seemed to take for granted. Her album and career represented what it felt like to be both praised and punished for a gifted ability. Her album represented what it meant to acknowledge being misunderstood as part of the miseducation, and as an opportunity for liberation. My own process of awareness, acknowledgment, and liberation came during one of the most difficult educational experiences of my life, my doctoral journey, and placed me on a path to my own acceptance of my gifts. In fact, being a doctoral student made me aware of the ways I had been miseducated, and through this, facilitated my unlearning about my own educational experiences, and engaged me in my relearning process. In this chapter, I am going to share my journey as an exceptionally gifted Black woman navigating a doctoral program. I will draw on the concept of miseducation from Woodson (2012) and Hill (1998), as well as the concepts of unlearning and relearning in Dillard (2012) and in adinkra symbolism (Willis, 1998) to discuss my process. I will conclude with a letter to exceptionally gifted Black girls and women and those who know them.

Making Things Hard

I guess I could say being "gifted" runs in my family. I was born and raised in Georgia, the second of four children. My mother was originally from Mississippi and moved to Georgia after marrying my father. She was the first in her family to attend and graduate from college. My father was from Georgia and finished an engineering degree (the second in his family to attend college) a couple of years before meeting my mother. My parents met at a national church convention, got engaged after my mom finished college, and married a few months later. My mother became a teacher at the parochial school where I would eventually attend and graduate from; my father helped run the family business of concrete subcontracting. My parents were smart, and their brilliance was contagious. They read a lot and had engaging conversations. As a family, we played lots of trivia games and enjoyed watching Jeopardy together. My parents cultivated an environment of curiosity and critical thinking; they bought encyclopedia sets, books, and worksheets. The answer to any question could be sourced.

My father was identified as gifted when he integrated into the middle school in his hometown. During that time, being accelerated (e.g., skipping grades) was a strategy for children like my dad, and he graduated from high school at 16. Similarly, my mother was identified as advanced and participated in Honors classes, honing in on her lifelong love and affinity for math. Along with my extended family, my parents heavily encouraged education as something that could never be taken away. I internalized early on that education, especially the ability to self-regulate learning, was part of my gifted ability. When my cousins and sister entered school before me, they were identified as gifted; my sister even tested out of kindergarten. Therefore, when I matriculated to my church's parochial school, I remember my extended family's assumptions that I would repeat the same pattern. Listening to church and family members' conversations, I internalized that I had to do well on this ability/gifted test. It would begin a pattern of internalizing the term gifted as being a problem and making things hard.

Tell Me Who I Have To Be

If you were to go back to my five-year-old self and ask her about the test, she would say that she did not do very well. I tested as gifted but not enough to skip kindergarten. I learned two things from this first gifted assessment. First, I learned that the term gifted is something given to you by some external authority. You cannot just call yourself gifted, it is an external identification or marker that is put on you. Second, I learned that there are levels to being gifted. I was gifted, but not gifted enough to skip grades like my sister. I internalized that I did not do well enough to be considered as smart as my sister. This internalization coupled with a love of learning and curiosity for the world around me, pushed me into high achievement. The school's curriculum was self-paced, and learners set daily goals monitored by the teachers. When a learner needed help or permission to pass a certain part of the work, they requested it. Otherwise, they completed their goals and took any material home with them that was not completed for the day. I completed my goals for the day and took material home to complete. By the time I was nine, I was identified as a new level of gifted: Advanced for my age cohort.

Over a period of four years, I completed enough academic work that would put me ahead almost into high school-level material. This meant that there would need to be some changes to account for my academic achievement. The following year, I was moved to my correct grade level – two years ahead of my age cohort. My peer group shifted significantly. I was now going to lunch and recess with those who were 2–5 years older than me. I had to socially adjust quickly, or at least try to. At the same time, my academic work was closely monitored, with the expectation that I would not complete more academic work than was assigned. I was no longer allowed to take any academic work home to complete. When I completed my assigned work for the day, I was permitted to bring in outside books and learning materials, or to be a helper to other educators in other grade levels. While this was all presented as a reward for my high achievement, I saw it as a punishment for making things hard.

Not long after these changes, my mother got me a book on what it meant to be gifted. In reading the book, I realized that there was a concept for my experience and that because of the way I saw the world, I was exceptional to others. The gifted label had changed my identity with those around me. My family saw me as a model child who was exceeding their academic expectations and gearing up for high achievement. My educators saw me as an ideal student, who did not need much attention, and whom they could direct to help other students. My peers saw me as a resource for ideas and to help with school work. I saw myself fragmented through each of their lenses and struggled with upholding the perceptions of others. If you told me who I had to be, I became that. The gifted label signaled a disjointed sense of self and contributed to my miseducation.

Becoming Miseducated: Primary and Secondary School Experiences

I first heard the term miseducation from one of the greatest albums of all time: *The Miseducation of Lauryn Hill*. The album was released on my thirteenth birthday and my father bought the cassette tape a couple of days after it was released. I was not allowed to listen to much music beyond Christian and Gospel music, so to be able to listen to this music was a bit of an anomaly in my household. I did not understand everything she talked about at the time, but I instantly connected with the theme of her having to learn things on her own. The album opens with a skit of a bell ringing in a classroom and a teacher calling roll. When he gets to her name – "Lauryn Hill. Lauryn Hill" – she does not answer. She is absent from the class on the day when they are learning everything she would discuss throughout the album. Themes of love, freedom, relationships, career, and family. She begins in the title track of the album (Hill, 1998, Track 14, Stanza 1) by describing what the miseducation feels like for her in the world: things moving fast, time moving along, and the weight of the pressure of the expectations of others. This miseducation, for me the label of gifted, had me internalizing messages about who I was and what I was supposed to be for others. For me, this meant that I was supposed to have knowledge about everything and be able to tutor others on any and every subject. When I did not have the right answer or say the right things, I felt like a failure because no matter what I attempted, I felt I could never meet the expectations of others for me. Everything I did felt like it was in vain. I began to believe the message that I was making things harder for myself just by being what everyone expected of me as a gifted individual.

Within the education space, Woodson (2012) popularized the term miseducation to describe how the educational system in the United States inadequately prepared Black people for the world in which they lived. Education, just like every other system, was racist and could not be leveraged for social mobility for Black people in its current form. Cooper (2016) added the layer of gender in her analysis of educational opportunities for Black people: There could be no social uplift for Black people, without attention to Black women and their education. Being a gifted Black woman, then, was a contradiction: the racist system both uplifts and praises me as inferior and as an exception to other Black people. As scholars research the various forms of miseducation, the barriers to education for minoritized populations, and the ways in which we should approach their education, I am further marginalized, as the concept of being "at-risk," is not applied to my situation.

Still, I related to many narratives of miseducation. The educational systems in which I engaged were not built with me in mind. I was exceptional in the educational norms created around my peers. Differently from other conceptualizations of miseducation, my exceptionality was praised as a standard for which others could compare, but unfairly not reach. And within this miseducation, I struggled. I struggled to take my ideas that I could talk about at length and write them into a coherent argument. I struggled with breaking down abstract concepts that were so easy to understand into practical and accessible information for others. I struggled with preparing for tests and standardized exams. I struggled with processing information that I had not read myself. I struggled with learning with others and building supportive peer networks for my educational success. I, too, was wholly underprepared for the world in the ways I had been miseducated.

These beliefs did not all arrive at once, but happened over time. When I asked for help or did not understand a topic, I learned quickly that I should figure things out on my own. My teachers would tell me, "you know how to do this" or, "come on, this is easy for you." For exceptionally gifted folks, I have now learned that we tend to understand abstract concepts well, but struggle with making those concepts concrete (Lovecky, 1994). From the perception of others, though, exceptionally gifted individuals should know it all if they understand the concept in general. For example, there was a common math module where we learned how to make change from purchases. The task was to first determine how much change was needed and then to determine how to distribute the change using U.S. currency. I struggled with this module and had to repeat it over and over again. I had the correct amount that was supposed to come in change, but when it came to the currency part, I kept getting the number of dollars and coins incorrect. My teacher was patient, but confused, and coached me the way I have become used to coaching and advice: "You are smart, you got the amount you need right, you are just using the incorrect denominations to arrive at your answer. Just sit and think about it. You can do it." I felt so ashamed and frustrated that I could not figure it out. Finally, I was helping another student with the module who was struggling with the subtracting part. I told them very honestly that I did not know what to do next, as I kept getting it wrong. We worked together to try to figure it out and in working with him, I saw that the correct answer was not just to come up with the exact change amount, but to use the least amount of dollars and coins as possible.

I learned and internalized three things from that experience. First, I could not rely on educators to know how to assist me when I did not know something. The gifted label prevented them from seeing me as a person who needed help. Second, I would need to find my own ways to make sense of things I did not understand. I internalized that when I had an issue, I had to find my own way to an answer, even if unto failure. Third, I learned how critical peer-learning would be in my educational experience. My peers became a source of knowledge, especially as it related to the particulars of learning where I was able to explain how things fit together. Quickly, I adapted to this way of learning: work until I reached a point where I did not know something, find ways to make meaning of this issue, and then rely on peers to help me to put the steps together. This would be my pattern of self-regulating my learning throughout my educational career. Like Ms. Hill, I was wholly underprepared for the world in the ways I had been miseducated. The implications of this would be clear upon my entering college at the age of fifteen.

Being Miseducated: Post-Secondary Experiences

A couple of weeks after enrolling in college, I celebrated my sixteenth birthday. I had made a small group of friends and they got me a cake for my birthday. When one of my friends asked me how old I was, I told her without thinking. She stared and then asked me again. I repeated myself, but slower this time, not realizing that I had revealed something that I thought I had left in a previous life. On the campus of about 1,000 students, the word spread quickly. Folks in my class asked to study with me and to proofread their papers. They asked me for help with complex problems and consulted me on how to say certain things. They did not believe me when I said I did not know and that I could not help. I could not talk openly about my struggles with attention, managing my time, retaining information, or writing. For the first time in my life, I received a grade below a B. I had faculty refer me to the writing center. I had faculty tell me that I could not write well and that they were concerned with my continuing. While the moniker of exceptionally gifted was great to be known on campus, my miseducation caught up to me in college.

I remember in my sophomore year, I was taking a standard math class for the Pre-Med track. The class was very difficult and I found myself for the first time seeking assistance from my advisor, given that I had not performed well on the first two tests. In our conversation, he convinced me to drop the class but that I would need to repeat it. This would mean that I would be knocked off course – I was on the Pre-Med track and had an undeclared major. I would not be able to graduate with my peers if I chose to do a science major. I told no one about this but my advisor. At the end of my sophomore year though, we had a new plan of action: I would declare myself as part of a pilot group of students to be a biopsychology major and, if I took courses over the next two summers, I could graduate on time with my peers. While this renewed me, it was the beginning of a series of realizations that coalesced into feelings of not being good enough. As I completed my studies, my advisor gave me one more piece of advice: he suggested that I change my career path to something he had seen me take a keen interest in: higher education.

A Miseducated Educator

I took his advice to heart. I had been an involved student during my time in college getting to experience things outside of academics for fulfillment. I enjoyed being involved in student government, being a resident assistant, a thrower for track and field, a manager for the volleyball team, and engaging in the local community through service. After my father got sick my senior year in college, I moved back home and worked in social services for two years. After two years, I decided to return to school for a master's degree in college student affairs administration. The familiar struggles of being in an educational environment resurfaced. My contributions in class discussions signaled to my professors and fellow students that I was different. When my classmates put together my age and graduation from college, there was even more of a perception that I was smarter than everyone. They did not see me struggling to keep track of readings, assignments, and projects. They were not aware of how long it took me to even complete assignments. In one of our assignments, we were supposed to take an issue in higher education and create enhancement ideas for the issues at a symposium. When I showed up, my classmates had these elaborate project boards and handouts for the invited students, faculty, and staff. All I had was a printout of the paper I had written, struggling to explain my ideas about diversity and inclusion in higher education, without visual aids.

Yet, I persisted and completed my master's degree on time. After graduation, I worked at two different universities in two varying functional areas. In each position, I was lauded for my great ideas, excellent implementation, and collaborative spirit. In private, I struggled with perfectionism, stereotype threat, and imposter syndrome (Anderson & Martin, 2018). I had high anxiety when I needed to present or prepare for a program. This was especially heightened when I needed to write reports or briefings for my projects. The same issues that I had in my past educational experiences were enhanced as an administrator. I was in a never-ending cycle of doing as much as I could and getting as far ahead in a project, and then seeking out help from colleagues who would not judge what I thought were inadequacies.

After working for almost two years as an administrator, I decided to get a doctorate. This surprised no one and was in line with what so many people "thought of me" (Hill, 1998, stanza 1). A couple of weeks into the first semester of my doctoral journey, I was contemplating making things hard for myself by dropping out. After quitting my job to go full-time, going through orientation, meeting with my advisor, and attending my first few classes, a familiar feeling began to surface. It was related to the pressure of the gifted label and the feelings of isolation and perfectionism. I internalized the message that I needed to be and do something that no one has ever done before. The pressure that I created for myself was too much and the instant relief of just quitting seemed to be ideal.

I did not quit on my doctoral journey. The day I contemplated quitting graduate school, I was on a bus heading home. I was consumed by my own thoughts, but a friendly voice invited me into conversation. Along the ride, we discussed both being doctoral students in education and the stress of being in our programs. As my friend departed, she invited me to come to a meeting where I would meet other minoritized graduate students and build my network. I later learned that my new associate's name was Jamil and she was the president of an organization for minoritized graduate students. I attended the first meeting some days later and left the meeting having signed up for study sessions and to help with fundraising. Those study sessions and fundraising events gave me a social outlet with people who were going through the same thing that I was. I learned through this organization that many of the members were identified as gifted Black women and they were too feeling the pressure of expectation. Our time together became spaces where we could lament, and offer advice to each other about navigating the doctoral journey. For the first time in my educational career, I felt supported and understood. This became an important site of unlearning for me in my doctoral journey: I did not have to do this educational experience as I had done others, I could do something different.

Unlearning My Miseducation

Unlearning is a concept that shows up in justice-oriented spaces as individuals become aware, interrogate, and deconstruct their biases around minoritized populations (Cochran-Smith, 2000). The process of unlearning can be jarring as individuals question perspectives that they have long held true and have to rebuild (Cochran-Smith, 2000). The unlearning process can further be hindered by the resistance of the individual to the need to change and possible regression in development (Cochran-Smith, 2000). At the intersection of being a Black gifted woman, my unlearning meant that I would have to resolve aspects of my identity and internalized expectations that I had long accepted as true. For example, the label of gifted came with its own set of expectations and rules from others that I internalized for myself. Namely, being a gifted Black woman meant that I was somehow set apart from other Black women and people. The pressure to have answers to all the questions and know how to do everything was a consistent part of my time as a doctoral student. For example, when doing group work with colleagues for class, I was always asked point blankly, "You're the smart one, what do you think we should do?" And I felt compelled to come up with the answers for the group. Within the doctoral journey, I unlearned many of these messages about the education process.

One of the implications of my being labeled gifted and the messages I internalized, was the isolation I felt in educational spaces. I felt the confusion of both not being able to ask for help and not being able to frame what support I needed. This is consistent with research on gifted students at various levels who do well academically but struggle socially (Fries-Britt, 1998; Fries-Britt & Griffin, 2007; Hébert & McBee, 2007). Scholars credit educational support services like student organizations, honors programs, and scholars programs as sites for social support that many students rely on, especially minoritized students (Fries-Britt & Griffin, 2007; Hébert & McBee, 2007). The isolation that I experienced was effectively neutralized with the social outlet of this organization and opened me up to how social support networks can be key to educational success.

Another important message unlearning was the need to overachieve, or be perfect to prove myself worthy of the gifted label. I risked dropping out of graduate school to avoid the increasing pressure of going above and beyond the requirements. I often overcommitted myself between and within projects. For example, one of the requirements in my program was to complete a pilot study. I developed the plan for the study and assembled a committee that approved my study to move forward. In discussion with my advisor about the research taking longer than expected, she remarked that my pilot study could have been a full dissertation study. As I reflected on that situation, I realized it was an important lesson on how to take the ideas that I have and make them more manageable.

Finally, I had to unlearn the negative self-talk that accompanied the internalized messages I developed over time about being gifted. This negative self-talk manifested as depression and anxiety for me. Like many other graduate students, my mental health suffered even more with the responsibilities and expectations I placed on myself as a doctoral student. Increasingly, mental health is becoming an important consideration for graduate students as they navigate the pressing demands of their educational process (Evans et al., 2018). Unlearning the coping mechanisms I developed over time led me to a therapist whose specialty was with individuals who experienced challenges related to being a gifted person. Talk therapy helped me to identify triggers for the negative self-talk, investigate patterns of behaviors that led to these triggers, and consider alternatives to these learned behaviors. Often when faced with a challenge during the doctoral process, I would rely on my default behaviors, which were preventing me from living a happy and whole life. Those behaviors stemmed from wanting a project to be perfect, so procrastination, not asking for help or clarification, and underperforming on class work ensued.

Unlearning was an incredible first step after becoming aware of my miseducation. While challenging to do, especially within a doctoral process, unlearning patterns of behaviors that kept me from fully engaging in my education was critical to my success as a doctoral student. Without unlearning, I most certainly would have dropped out of graduate school and continued to operate within my miseducation. As I unlearned, a parallel process was also unfolding where I was reimagining and relearning my own way of being in educational spaces as a gifted Black woman. This took me to an entirely new context to relearn and reconnect with my own way of being. I would need to go to another country to begin my own relearning process.

Nea Onnim No Sua A, Ohu: Relearning and (Re)membering

My first two years as a doctoral student centered on becoming aware of my miseducation as a gifted Black woman, and unlearning so many ways of being that impacted how I engaged with educational spaces. Consequently, as I entered my third year, I felt a disconnect from everything around me. One of the impacts of unlearning is a feeling that nothing is known and everything is relative. I would participate in class discussions, research projects, and with friends, but with a constant feeling of disassociating. I made it through my pilot study with the help of my advisor to streamline, submit, and present the final paper to my committee. I began the next uphill battle of preparing for my comprehensive exams. I was hoping to continue my pilot study on socialization for new professionals within my field when I got an email that would significantly alter my life. The organization that had been pivotal in helping me to reorient toward social networks was advertising a study abroad trip to Ghana, West Africa in education. The lead for the trip was Dr. Cynthia Dillard, a professor at the university I attended at the time. Dillard was one of my favorite educational researchers, that centered Black women educators and academics in her work. Further, she posited the Endarkened Feminist Epistemology that guides this volume. I knew from that initial email that I needed to go to Ghana.

In December 2015, I boarded a plane for my third trip outside of the United States to Ghana. I had taken and successfully defended my comprehensive exams, and I was tired. The stress of navigating the doctoral experience and unlearning so many things related to my educational experience overwhelmed me. However, those ten days that I spent in Ghana, gave me an incredible boost of energy that has not waned. I learned about the history of Ghana and its connections to the United States. I learned about how that history and culture influenced the educational system, as well as the impacts of colonialism and neocolonialism. There was so much to understand, but I gravitated toward one cultural element in particular: adinkra symbols.

Adinkra symbols are pictorial representations of value-based concepts and proverbs within Ghanaian culture. Each symbol has a name in the local Ghanaian language of Twi which, when translated into English also contains important wisdom for consideration.

My favorite adinkra symbol is the symbol *Nea Onnim No Sua A, Ohu*, which translates to "he or she who does not know can learn through teaching." It became my mantra for the phase of my doctoral journey as an exceptionally gifted Black woman that I call relearning. For everything I had to unlearn about education – social support for learning, overachievement and perfection, and negative self-talk – I had to relearn new ways of being and operating. On the trip and in her writings, Dillard (2012) centers the notion of (re)membering ways of knowing and being within the global tradition of being Black and African. Within (re)membering, Dillard stresses engaging in the cultural and spiritual practices that reconnects Black people with themselves and their cultural heritage. My time in Ghana introduced me to this process and to the incredible opportunity to have a framework for my relearning.

Relearning with Others

In previous educational experiences, I had internalized my gifted label to mean that my learning was an individual process that only I was responsible for. In (re)membering, I relearned that learning is a social process. For Black people, the community of learning would be critical in my doctoral journey. Throughout my doctoral journey, I met some incredible individuals who became part of my community of learning. They helped me think through ideas, they became research and practice collaborators, and they were my accountability for completing my doctoral journey. I relearned how to be with others in a learning process that has continued following graduation. From Jamil's conversation on the bus to the writing of this chapter, the relearning with others has been critical to my success, and my own understanding of my learning process.

Relearning Authenticity

Hill (1998) went through a similar process as she attended to her own miseducation. She started to trust herself more and see herself as the source of her success rather than others. In the chorus of *Miseducation*, Hill has a realization about knowing in her heart that she already had the answer within her and that she could define her own destiny" (Hill, 1998, Stanza 3). The doctoral journey was an important impetus for my own process of being authentic to myself and to my own thoughts. The gifted label does not have to mean what others think, it means that I may approach things differently than others. I may make simple things harder than it needs to be, but it is part of my gift and how I approach the world. The answer to the question of how to approach my life is within me.

Message to Those Who Know Exceptionally Gifted Black Girls and Women

Thank you for reading. I hope I have provided a perspective on how I navigated the world, but especially my doctoral journey as an exceptionally gifted Black woman. If you were reading this, and someone came to mind, I invite you to consider how your past interactions may have impacted this person. As you consider these interactions, I invite you to think of ways that any future interactions with exceptionally gifted Black girls and women will focus on who they are as a person, rather than how you expect them to be. They only know their own version of normal, so give them room to show you who they are and resist the urge to make them feel like who they are naturally is a problem. For us, how we think and how we are is the only way that we know, and because it is different from most, there is already an isolating feeling. And if you are lucky to know multiple exceptionally gifted Black girls and women, find ways to connect them with each other, so that they know that they are not alone.

Message to My Fellow Exceptionally Gifted Black Women

I hope that I have shared something in this chapter that you connect with, given our shared identity. If you have carried the weight of any messages related to the label of being gifted, I hope you see my story as confirmation that it can get better. Your whole self matters, not just the gifted parts. You matter not because of your gift; your gift is a bonus that you get to use to bless the world in your own way. I think that becoming aware of the ways that you have been miseducated and committing to unlearning and relearning how to engage in the world as a gifted person is difficult, but possible. When I attended to the messages I had internalized about myself and my gifts, I experienced an immense relief that has freed me to live on and with purpose. Further, I have been able to see the ways that my gifts benefit me, and identify ways that I can get better over time. I hope the same for you. You got this. *Nea Onnim No Sua A, Ohu.*

References

Anderson, B. N., & Martin, J. A. (2018). What K–12 teachers need to know about teaching gifted Black girls battling perfectionism and stereotype threat. *Gifted Child Today*, 41(3), 117–124.

Angelou, M. (1991). *All god's children need traveling shoes*. Vintage.
Angelou, M. (1997). *I know why the caged bird sings*. Bantam.
Brown, B. (2015). *Daring greatly: How the courage to be vulnerable transforms the way we live, love, parent, and lead*. Penguin.
Butler, O. E. (2012). *Parable of the sower*. Open Road Media.
Cochran-Smith, M. (2000). Blind vision: Unlearning racism in teacher education. *Harvard Educational Review*, 70(2), 157–190.
Collins, P. H. (2002). *Black feminist thought: Knowledge, consciousness, and the politics of empowerment*. Routledge.
Cooper, A. J. (2016). *A voice from the south*. Dover Publications.
Crenshaw, K. (2017). *On intersectionality: Essential writings*. The New Press.
Dillard, C. B. (2012). *Learning to (re) member the things we've learned to forget: Endarkened feminisms, spirituality, and the sacred nature of research and teaching*. Peter Lang.
Evans, T. M., Bira, L., Gastelum, J. B., Weiss, L. T., & Vanderford, N. L. (2018). Evidence for a mental health crisis in graduate education. *Nature Biotechnology*, 36(3), 282–284.
Fries-Britt, S. (1998). Moving beyond Black achiever isolation: Experiences of gifted Black collegians. *The Journal of Higher Education*, 69(5), 556–576.
Fries-Britt, S., & Griffin, K. (2007). The Black box: How high-achieving Blacks resist stereotypes about Black Americans. *Journal of College Student Development*, 48(5), 509–524.
Gross, M. U. M. (1999). Small poppies: Highly gifted children in the early years. *Roeper Review*, 21(3), 207–214.
Hébert, T. P., & McBee, M. T. (2007). The impact of an undergraduate honors program on gifted university students. *Gifted Child Quarterly*, 51(2), 136–151.
Hill, L. (1998). *The miseducation of Lauryn Hill [album]*. [Philadelphia, Pennsylvania], Ruffhouse.
Lorde, A. (1982). *Zami: A new spelling of my name*. Crossing Press.
Lovecky, D. V. (1994). Exceptionally gifted children: Different minds. *Roeper Review*, 17(2), 116–120.
Morgan, J. (2018). *She Begat This: 20 Years of The miseducation of Lauryn Hill*. Simon and Schuster.
Walker, A. (2004). *In search of our mothers' gardens: Womanist prose*. Houghton Mifflin Harcourt.
Walker, A. (2011). *The color purple*. Open Road Media.
Walker, A. (2021). *We are the ones we have been waiting for: Inner light in a time of darkness*. The New Press.
Willis, W. B. (1998). *The Adinkra dictionary: A visual primer on the language of Adinkra*. Pyramid Complex.
Woodson, C. G. (2012). *The miseducation of the Negro*. Start Publishing, LLC.

3
IT TAKES A VILLAGE
Cultivating Belonging, Community, and Sisterhood

Joan Collier, Ph.D.

Introduction

I have always loved learning. School was where I learned course content and learned about life. I often made friends with other kids and people who enjoyed learning. I was considered bright, not gifted, but the absence of a gifted designation did not stop teachers from nurturing my intellect. As an adult learner, particularly as a doctoral student, being in community with other Black women learners and supportive faculty championed my intelligence and my own understanding of myself as a high ability learner; A girl has range. Being in community with other brilliant sista-scholars, encouraging family and friends, and supportive faculty aided me in releasing residual doubts about my own intelligence from earlier in life. Belonging to a community of high-achieving scholars with different associations to gifted status affirmed that regardless of our gifted designation in earlier life, we were all extraordinarily talented.

Our stories are ones of oppression and resistance (Collins, 2000). In (re)membering that we have survived and learned to thrive, in spite of ongoing racialized and gendered violence (Dillard, 2012), I wrote this chapter so that other Black women interested in or currently pursuing a doctorate could witness what is possible when sista-scholars have a sense of belonging and a strong community during the doctoral process. I wrote this chapter almost six years post-Ph.D., and I am still somewhat tender from that journey, but I am healing. Besides degree attainment, my balm has been the fortified personal and professional relationships I gained during that time with other sista-scholars.

Sense of Belonging

Within higher education, Schlossberg (1985) provided a theoretical framework for making sense of the experiences of mattering and marginality that university administrators and faculty could draw upon to facilitate community building and promote belonging among college students. Through a more transformative lens, Strayhorn (2012) emphasized the exacerbated impact of belonging, and its absence, on academic achievement and social wellness for Black students, students of color, and students with marginalized identities. As a college student affairs professional, I understood belonging in theoretical and realized ways, since my job required that I facilitate community building and foster belonging for undergraduate students, within my professional capacity. This knowledge and skill set served me well as a doctoral student in building networks that would enable me to survive and thrive.

Endarkened Feminist Epistemology

Epistemologies are ways of knowing (Guba & Lincoln, 2005). *Endarkened Feminist Epistemology* (Dillard, 2006) is a way of knowing that recognizes the ways in which Black women make meaning through lived experiences and know themselves more accurately through dialogue and in-community conversation. Blended from feminist and African diasporic ways of knowing, Endarkened Feminist Epistemology (EFE) honors dialogical learning, legitimizes lived experiences, names care as a responsibility within a community, and affirms the role of spirituality, or connectedness, within research.

Assumption 1: Self-definition forms one's participation and responsibility to one's community.
Assumption 2: Research is both an intellectual and a spiritual pursuit, a pursuit of purpose.
Assumption 3: Only within the context of community does the individual appear (Palmer, 1983) and, through dialogue, continue to become.
Assumption 4: Concrete experience within everyday life form the criterion of meaning, the "matrix of meaning making" (Ephraim-Donker, 1997, p. 8).
Assumption 5: Knowing and research are both historical (extending backwards in time) and outward to the world: To approach them otherwise is to diminish their cultural and empirical meaningfulness.
Assumption 6: Power relations, manifest as racism, sexism, homophobia, and so on structure gender, race, and other identity relations within research (pp. 18–27).

EFE was a gift to my emerging researcher identity and a beautifully brilliant complement to the belonging framework I used to make sense of connection making and community building. EFE aided me in belonging to myself as a Black woman. I knew we knew things by experiencing them, and through our bodies, but that knowledge had rarely, if ever, been acknowledged or affirmed during my formal education. EFE was a framework for (re)membering and honoring intuitive knowledge that was often doubted out of me throughout educational systems that valued objectivity by disparaging subjectivity and embodied knowing. Other Black feminisms and critical theories named systems of oppression that helped me to better articulate structural, epistemological, and ontological violence that shaped my experiences as a Black person, a woman, and as a Black woman.

My framework for belonging gained depth when undergirded by an Endarkened Feminist Epistemological framing. How I saw and understood people and how I sought to be known by others was enriched. I sought to be known and belong in my fullness, and I set out to know others more fully. Belonging was known in my gut, intuitively, through spirit. Community became any gathering where truth could be spoken in love and with care, listening was done with the intent to understand and know, and connection and collaboration were prioritized over competition.

These are my stories.

CSAA (cuh-sah)

I chose the College Student Affairs Administration (CSSA) program in the College of Education for two reasons: faculty support and a compositionally diverse student body within the program. Both enabled my ability to succeed, which I knew was dependent, in part, on my sense of belonging and ability to be a part of a thriving scholarly community.

Graduate student socialization is centered around the academic program and professional capacity building more than institutional identity or interpersonal development (Weidman et al., 2001). Because of this orientation to the graduate experience, the academic program home, aspirant or chosen industry culture, and faculty and peer interactions can impact and inform a sense of belonging along the spectrum of marginality and mattering for graduate students, particularly students from minoritized backgrounds, including Black women in historically white institutional spaces. Program faculty who had been thoughtful advisors through my master's experience had worked diligently to recruit me back for my doctoral experience. With their support, I knew that I would be okay there, despite my ongoing frustrations with the university's broader culture. New faculty had joined the program and brought with them critical perspectives that would change the way I analyzed the world around me.

The other reason I chose CSAA was because of the network of Black students in the doctoral program, what we Black folks affectionately named *Black CSAA*. As master's students, Black CSAA members affirmed us, cheered us on, and made sure to check in on the five Black women in my cohort: Roshaunda, Jemilia, Tasha, Jillian, and me (Joan Collier). As a new doctoral student, the current Black CSAA welcomed me with open arms, chief among them, Jillian, my master's-cohort mate. CSAA's racial demographic composition made it an outlier in that half of the program's students were Black identified. At one time during my studies, there were approximately fifteen Black doctoral students at various stages of the doctoral process in the program. I knew what I was experiencing was what Schlossberg called mattering (1985). People knew me, knew my name, cared to ask how I was doing, extended themselves and their networks to me, and affirmed my capacity as a scholar. In spite of the broader institutional climate, I knew that on the fourth floor of our college of education, I was cared for and mattered.

Learning to (Re)member

I (re)member wanting to change up my courses to learn more about concepts and ideas that I believed would transform my understanding of the world and better inform my research. A study abroad in Ghana, West Africa facilitated a deeper belonging that I had been yearning for as an ascendant of enslaved Africans in the United States. Depending on which branch of the family tree I examined and what we were able to maintain through written and oral histories, I understand myself to be five or six generations removed from US chattel slavery. On both sides of the family, I am the first generation removed from Jim Crow segregation. I had a strong racial identity and wanted to deepen that by connecting my Black identity to a broader Black cultural experience in West Africa.

The cohort of all Black doctoral students, program staff, and faculty would spend the winter session in Ghana, West Africa with Dr. Cynthia B. Dillard, Distinguished Professor of Education and Queen Mother in Mpeasem, as our teacher and guide. We spent the fall semester readying ourselves to engage in (re)membering, the process of identifying where we belong, unpacking how we forgot, and honoring our fullness by reclaiming who we are as African ascendant people (Dillard, 2012). Preparation entailed learning about pre-colonial and present-day Ghanaian cultures and histories and unlearning romanticized ideas of the African continent.

We became a tight-knit community over the course of our semester-long preparation course and during our travels. Learning in community, with the people we met there, through site visits to local landmarks with Diasporic significance (e.g., Final Bath, Cape Coast, Slave Castle, etc.), and through the shared histories and present realities of people of African ascent shaped our time in Ghana. Two of my program faculty and a program mate were a part of the experience, which provided additional support as the cohort grappled with our relationships as Black Americans with the land, cultures, and people of West Africa. The daily process of (re)membering was facilitated by Dr. Dillard's invitation to reflect on the question, "What does/did Ghana have to teach us?" and the cohort engaging in dialogue, listening eagerly to what others learned to see how that person's knowledge might inform what we were learning for ourselves.

My pastor said that we were always with ourselves (Callahan, personal communication, 2019), and the Ghana Study Abroad in Education experience (re)minded me of who I was across time, geography, and ancestry. I returned to campus feeling a deeper connection to the broader Diaspora and the cohort I traveled with, equipped to begin healing from wounds of intraracial conflict resulting from the lies of white supremacy and internalized anti-blackness, excited about the possibilities for improved community dialogue and connection between African ascendant people, and committed to an endarkened feminist epistemological lens as a researcher and community member. Adopting the practice of (re)membering solidified my sense of self and belonging within the Diasporic community, and that expanding sense of belonging brought me tremendous comfort, pride, and enthusiasm to learn more about other connections across the Diaspora.

The Ghana Study Abroad In Education experience deepened my sense of belonging as a member of the African Diaspora as an African American and moved me to adopt an Endarkened Feminist Epistemology for living and research that shaped my research and continues to impact the way I navigate the world.

Sista-Scholars and Sista Circles

I adopted the term sista-scholar from another sista-scholar somewhere along the doctoral journey. I valued the term's affirming and aspirational descriptors of who I knew us to be. We were sistas, Black women in the academy, and we were scholars, an aspiration and fact. Sista-scholars were vital to my success as a doctoral student, from program recruitment to post-graduation job placement. In a more systemized way, sista circles were formal and informal networks of Black women that relied on mutuality to aid in the support of Black women to achieve desired outcomes (e.g., sense of belonging, community building and support, mutual aid and care, research, etc.) (Neal-Barnett et al., 2011). Leveraging these networks enabled me to succeed academically and socially and allowed me to reflect and share back the love, care, and support that had been so generously shared with me by sista-scholars. According to hooks 2000, p. 129) "Communities sustain life- not nuclear families, or the "couple," and certainly not the rugged individualist. There is no better place to learn the art of loving than in community." Beyond my faculty, faith community, and family of origin and chosen families, sista-scholars and sista circles were a primary support network and structures as a doctoral student, in part, because they understood the trials and triumphs of the doctoral experience in ways that many people in my established communities did not.

While a large contingency of sista-scholars was in my program, sista-scholars represented a variety of disciplines and academic programs. For many of the sista-scholars not in my program, they were an "only" or one of a few in their program or department. Additionally, the programs and departments demonstrated limited capacities for supporting Black women as scholars or as racialized and gendered people. In earlier work, hooks stated "Collective unmasking is an important act of resistance. If it remains a mark of our oppression that as Black people we cannot be dedicated to truth in our lives, without putting ourselves at risk, then is it a mark of our resistance, our commitment to liberation, when we claim the right to speak the truth of our reality anyway (1993, pp. 16–17)" In personal communications, sista-scholars shared experiencing overt and subtle indignities related to and at the intersection of race and gender in and out of the classroom. Spaces we created for ourselves, sista circles, were where we could tell our truths, be heard, have our pains and joys witnessed, and be our more authentic selves.

Several of us were developing or deepening our identities as Black feminists. We were learning about liberation, equity, power, and a love ethic. Sista circles and being in community with sista-scholars was one way of developing a praxis around those ideas. Through Black feminism, I learned to heal and speak more truthfully. Healing required the truth about myself and our collective self. In community with sista-scholars, I began unlearning the respectability politic (Cooper, 2017) that had shaped so much of my life as a professional and a person. I began shaping a liberation-focused politic. We were working out our truths, angsts, inconsistencies, and aspirations in community with one another in a way that we were often unable to in other settings. Being in community with sista-scholars and sista circles provided the psychological safety that enabled us to practice truth-telling and authenticity in ways that deepened my sense of belonging to the community and myself.

Sista-scholars regularly asked each other questions about basic needs: "Sis, did you eat?", "Are you drinking your water", "Did you stretch today?", "Have you talked with someone who loves you outside of school lately?" These supposedly simple questions were one way of showing care and reminding each other that we are our sisters' keepers. Lorde's quote, (1988) "Caring for myself is not self-indulgence. It is self-preservation, and that is an act of political warfare." about self-care was trendy during our time in graduate school, but my sista-scholar networks took it more seriously than its superficial capitalist interpretation. In practice, self-care was tied to community care, the well-being of the whole. To care for ourselves, we had shared meals to ensure folks actually ate, hosted writing and reading sessions to provide support for folks who needed to write but did not want to be alone for hours and days on end, created space for celebration of the mundane and momentous, and made sure that folks had what they needed when they were unwell.

Sista circles are predicated on existing relationships or connections and a shared aim. We were all in school to earn our doctorates: graduation was the end game. Seeing each other win was a joy. My sister's win is my win. Accountability looked like checking in on people who had missed writing time or who had gone silent in the group chat—not to shame them, but to see how they were doing and to see how we could support them toward our shared goal. The semester before we were aiming to defend and graduate, a sista-scholar asked about how my dissertation work was coming along. I shared with her how exhausted I was and that I did not know if I would be able to rally in time for a spring defense. Before I could continue, she looked me dead in my face and said, "WE are graduating in May. We. Us. Let us know what support you need because we are all getting out of here in the spring." When my mentor died suddenly of cancer that spring, those same sista-scholars rallied to support me as I grieved my way to graduation that May.

Sista-scholar Marvette and I were program mates and close friends. Both of us employed Sista Circle Methodology (Johnson, 2015) in our dissertations that had examined and explored varied aspects of Black graduate women's experiences and identity at a historically white institution. Through our research and personal experience, we valued the community building and belonging that sista circles fostered for Black women. We partnered together to host a series of sista circles for Black graduate women at our home institution to expand the practice of purposefully creating community through sista circles for the sista-scholars who would remain on campus beyond our graduation. Sista circle gatherings aimed to connect sista-scholars across programs to minimize isolation for the 'only's and one-of-a-fews' in their respective programs and departments, build a sense of belonging to a broader community of Black graduate women, engage in authentic and affirming dialogue, and create experiences that spiritually renewed sista-scholars.

We culminated the sista circle series with a photoshoot for participants and other Black graduate women who wanted to be a part of the experience. The aim was to create an embodied experience of belonging with other Black graduate women, so that when participants looked at the photos, they would be reminded that they were part of a large community of Black graduate women. We paid for the photoshoot ourselves so that cost was not a barrier to participation for anyone who wanted to be a part of the experience. That was one way for us to show sista-scholars that we cared about them and wanted them to see themselves as belonging to something larger. The shoot was fabulous, and the experience was successful in providing sista-scholars with an experience that affirmed their place at the university and as part of a bigger sista-scholar network.

Relationships with sista-scholars and sista circles deepened my sense of belonging by promoting authenticity and truth-telling, fostering reciprocity, and being a space of care and accountability. They were (and continue to be) my "life-affirming, counter-system for valuation", and for that, I am grateful.

Cite A Sista

I (re)member the day Sista-scholar Brittany Williams and I thought up #CiteASista. We were taking the whiteness and white supremacy in Higher Education course through our program and were required to craft a response project for class. Our aim in partnering together was to create a project that centered on and affirmed Black women. We defined #CiteASista

> As a digital counterspace, [where] we use #CiteASista as Black womxn to validate one another's experiences, highlight our erasure, and to call attention to new works by, for, and with Black womxn and girls. It is also a space where Black womxn faculty and graduate womxn in training can provide (co)mentorship and encouragement to one another along the journey.
>
> *(Williams & Collier, 2022)*

We created Cite A Sista (CAS) as a Black feminist project that promoted and advocated for the increased citation use of Black women's knowledge within and beyond the academy in 2016.

Using the #CiteASista, we hosted our first twitter chat that July. The sista-scholar and sista-scholar allied networks in and beyond CSAA supported us online by participating in the chat and engaging with posts through likes and retweets. What began as a course project, quickly transitioned into a digital community for Black women seeking community with other Black women. We leveraged engagement from Black women graduate students, higher education professionals, faculty, and Black women's allies within and beyond our program and school for monthly twitter chats that created communal space for the "only's" and "one-of-a-fews" in their program, and for Black women who did not see themselves represented in their program or department. Chats grew into a website with a Black women's blogging community where Black graduate women could connect and witness about their ideas and lived experiences with school, work, structural issues, parenting, partnership, and more. Fostering community digitally led to hosting in-person events at industry conferences for Black women in higher education and student affairs. Digital community members wanted to get to know the folks they had been chatting with online or whose blogs they had been following. I met new people at every conference and was often reminded that having a rich community, supported the belonging I had through Black CSAA and the sista-scholar network at my home campus. This was not the case for so many other Black women in graduate schools across the country, or even at my own institution.

In cultivating digital and in-person communities where folks saw themselves reflected was the commitment to a Black feminist space where liberation was the aim. The Cohambee River Collective (1978) offered that, "If Black women were free, it would mean that everyone else would have to be free since our freedom would necessitate the destruction of all the systems of oppression." We agreed, which meant that we all had work to do in unlearning ideas that diminished the worth of another or contributed to the oppression or discrimination of someone else. Monthly twitter chats promoted dialogue about multiple dimensions of experience, identity, and community learning and accountability (e.g., unpacking and combatting cissexism, parental status, navigating romantic partnership, citational politic and praxis, etc.). We wanted to cultivate spaces where Black women across identities could belong and work out their liberation in good company.

CAS cultivated a community that deepened my sense of belonging as part of academic discipline, with an extended network of Black women graduate students, faculty, and professionals and promoted belonging for Black women. Sense of belonging through this community empowered and enabled me to ground myself in the embodied work of CAS' praxis.

A Testament to Community

The Multicultural Services and Programs hosted the annual Rites of Passage (ROP), the pre-commencement celebration centering Black and African Diasporic graduates. These celebrations of joy and resistance are a common practice at historically white institutions with histories and legacies of racial exclusion. Families, friends, and community members come from near and far to wish the soon-to-be-graduates well and students take part in a ritual where invited loved ones drape a *kente* stole across their regalia.

The Multicultural Services and Programs (MSP), and its staff in particular, had been part of my community and a place of belonging during my masters and doctoral experiences at the university. As a master's student, I had been a practicum student in the African American Cultural Center which had been collapsed into the MSP by the time I returned for doctoral studies. I attended the Rites of Passage ceremony as a student earning my Master of Education alongside Jillian, Roshaunda, and Jemilia. As I prepared to graduate with my Ph.D, the MSP staff asked if I would be willing to give the keynote address for the Rites of Passage ceremony. I was thrilled to be considered and humbly accepted. Myself and other members with institutional knowledge advocated for the club to pay the ROP fees so that graduate students would be represented and get to experience this signature Black cultural celebration which meant that part of the sista-scholar crew would share in the ceremony as well.

My keynote was a love letter to and testimony about the power of belonging and community. I end this chapter with the words I used to conclude my doctoral experience.

> Earning my Ph.D. was one of the most challenging undertakings of my life. It took a village to get me through this process. There were my sibling-scholars who stayed up late and got up early to write with me, faculty members who encouraged my creativity and brilliance and told me to do better because they knew I had better in me, spiritual family who prayed for me when I was out of prayers to pray for myself, and kinfolk who didn't understand exactly what I was doing but who always had an encouraging word. I couldn't afford to have people in my village who kept negativity on their tongues or discord in their actions … Remember, it takes a village, which means that the people we surround ourselves with matters. Protect your village. Protect yourself. Choose wisely because … it takes a village.
>
> On this campus, I was a part of communities of Black graduate women, some of whom were the only Black person or Black woman in their academic program or department. I've already talked about

my village, but I recognized that some of my sista-scholars didn't have the village they wanted here. Together, Dr. Marvette Lacy and I, who is also graduating tomorrow, decided that we would host sista-circles for Black graduate women on this campus this past spring to help them create, expand, and celebrate the villages that they desired or had here. We hosted a photoshoot for fellow sista-scholars to remind each of them, and ourselves, that we had some agency to create or enhance a village."

To my fellow graduates, remember that it takes a village. Whatever your "it" is, it too requires a village. Because it takes a village, build your village thoughtfully, being sure to include people who can build you up and not tear you down. Because it takes a village, remember that you are part of your village and for that, reciprocity is a must. Give, care, share, and be active in your own village. Because it takes a village, build one when you lack one. Create it, because ... it takes a village.

Conclusion

This chapter detailed the impact of belonging and community on my doctoral experience and those of other sista-scholars navigating the challenges of graduate study and structural violence caused by white supremacy, patriarchy, and misogynoir. Like the title of Love's (2019) text, we want to do more than survive. Sista-scholars want and deserve to thrive. Sense of belonging positions sista-scholars, and all students, for success (Strayhorn, 2012; Schlossberg, 1985). Institutions that claim to value belonging, inclusion, and diversity have a responsibility to create environments where people marginalized by race and gender are empowered to thrive. In the presence and absence of institutional support, I encourage other sista-scholars to "make sure somebody care about you" (Grandma Johnnie Mae, personal communication). Seek out people, places, and experiences where you find belonging and be empowered to cultivate experiences and spaces for belonging and community where they do not yet exist.

References

Collective, C. R. (1977). 'A Black Feminist Statement' (pp. 210–218).*Cohambee River Collective Statement*. (1978).

Collins, P. H. (2000). *Black feminist thought: Knowledge, consciousness, and the politics of empowerment* (Rev. 10th anniversary ed.). Routledge.

Cooper, B. (2017). *Beyond respectability: The intellectual thought of race women*. University of Illinois Press.

Dillard, C. B. (2006). *On spiritual strivings: Transforming an African American woman's academic life*. State University of New York Press.

Dillard, C. B. (2012). *Learning to (re)member the things we've learned to forget: Endarkened feminism, spirituality, & the sacred nature of research & teaching*. Peter Lang.

Ephraim-Donker, A. (1997). *African spirituality: On becoming ancestors*. Trenton, NJ: Africa World Press.

Guba, E. G., & Lincoln, Y. S. (2005). Paradigmatic controversies, contradictions, and emerging confluences. In: Denzin, N. K. and Lincoln, Y.S., Eds., *The Sage Handbook of Qualitative Research*, 3rd Edition, Sage, Thousand Oaks, 191–215.

hooks, b. (1993 [2015]). *Sisters of the yam: Black women and self-recovery*. Routledge.

hooks, b. (2000). *All about love: New visions*. Harper Perenial.

Johnson, L. (2015). *Using sista circles to examine the professional experiences of contemporary Black women teachers in schools: A collective story*. (Unpublished doctoral dissertation). University of Georgia.

Lorde, A. (1988). *A burst of light: And other essays*. Firebrand Book.

Love, B. L. (2019). *We want to do more than survive: Abolitionist teaching and the pursuit of educational freedom*. Beacon Press.

Neal-Barnett, A. M., Stadulis, R., Payne, M. R., Crosby, L., Mitchell, M., Williams, L., & Williams-Costa, C. (2011). In the company of my sisters: Sister circles as an anxiety intervention for professional African American women. *Journal of Affective Disorders, 129*(1), 213–218.

Schlossberg, N. K. (1985). *Mattering and marginality: A lifespan approach*. Paper resented at the Annual Meeting of the American Psychological Association, Los Angeles, CA.

Strayhorn, T. L. (2012). *College students' sense of belonging: A key to educational success for all students*. Routledge.

Weidman, J. C., Twale, D. J., & Stein, E. L. (2001). Socialization of graduate and professional students in higher education: A perilous passage? In *ASHE-ERIC higher education report* (Vol. 28, pp. 25–54). Jossey-Bass.

Williams, B., & Collier, J. (2022). How #citeasista leveraged online platforms to center Black women. In B. T. Kelly & S. Fries-Britt (Eds.), *Building mentorship networks to support Black women: A guide to succeeding in the academy* (pp. 100–120). Routledge.

4

FACE YOUR STUDIES

Exploring Education, Opportunity, and Community as a First-Generation Immigrant

Funlola G. Are, Ph.D.

Introduction

"Face your studies" is a phrase so ingrained in my head, I will never forget it. In fact, it has now become somewhat of a personal mantra for me. A phrase I use to get myself going, whether I am getting pumped for the day ahead, or I catch myself staring into space getting lost in one of the million places my mind often takes me to. I snap myself out of it by whispering to myself, "face your studies," often followed by a gentle head shake to bring me back to reality. Although I have now adopted this phrase as my own, it often annoyed me growing up. Likely, due to when my parents used the phrase, it was in direct opposition to either what I was doing in the moment, or what I wanted to do. "Face your studies" was the phrase that rang out when my mom would catch me watching TV while I was supposed to be doing my homework, or when I would ask my dad to go to a party or over to a friend's house. "No, you need to face your studies." This was a household adage, repeated time and time again; especially as I got older. Now that I have reclaimed the phrase as my own personal assertion, it is a gentle reminder to get things done, and to work towards an end goal, whether educational or personal in nature. As I reflected on my doctoral journey in the text that follows, it seemed fitting that the title of these reflections mirror the words that served as the foundation of my upbringing, the goals my immigrant parents had for me, and the perseverance to navigate the program and its challenges. Through this chapter, I unpack what my doctoral journey meant to me as a Nigerian American first-generation immigrant who grew up with the constant reminder to "face your studies."

To ensure that we are all on the same page, I want to begin by operationalizing what it means to be a first-generation American. The term "first-generation" has been used both to mean a family's first generation of children born in the new home country (Owens & Lynch, 2012) as well as foreign-born individuals who are the first generation of their family to live in the United States and receive citizenship (United States Census Bureau, 2021). With that said, my parents are Nigerian immigrants who moved to Houston, Texas in the 1980s. My siblings and I are the first generation of children born in the United States to my family and I self-identify as first-generation. My parents, similar to many immigrants who traveled to the United States, were in search of advanced education opportunities for themselves and their future children.

As I reflect on how to contextualize my experiences as a Black woman and a first-generation American, it may not be the immigration narrative that is commonly amplified. I do not think of myself as having to navigate two different nationalities or feeling torn about embracing my Nigerian culture. I do not remember feeling boxed out or estranged from the culture of the United States, but rather, view myself as having a blended experience, an integration. One reason for that may be that when my parents immigrated to the United States, there was no language barrier for them. The official language in Nigeria was English and thus, my parents grew up speaking English and Yoruba (our native language). In fact, they often remarked that they spoke better English than me, which was likely the truth. When my parents immigrated to the United States, they had a support system here, a sibling, a cousin, and a friend they went to school with when they were in Nigeria. Therefore, this established network made their adjustment to the United States easier. Although they shared stories of how challenging things were for them, they equally shared stories of how they made it through these difficult times with family and close friends alongside them. I believe these experiences had a direct impact on the way that my parents raised my siblings and I. Family was a source of support, an unwavering community that I could always rely on, and it went beyond just my parents and siblings. It extended to distant relatives, and friends of friends. My parents believed in helping others, and my siblings and I grew up watching this.

Face Your Studies: Early Education and Socialization Experiences

As a Nigerian American, if I were to sum up the biggest influence of my identity on present-day achievement, it would be the emphasis on education. As mentioned, my parents came to the United States seeking better educational opportunities for their children, and consequently, this was commonly discussed. From a young age, my parents instilled the importance of education, and this became a key part of my identity as a young person and remains with me today as an academic scholar. I was expected to make A's, although, actually at that time it wasn't simply A's, it was 100/100. If I got lower than that, then my parents questioned me. For instance, if I made a 90 my parents would ask me why I didn't make a 100. I dare not say, "but my classmate made an 85 and my grade is better than his." If I did, my parents' favorite line was, "So you want to compare yourself to someone who did worse than you?" They instilled in me that I should strive to be at the top of my class, but not in a way in which I was competing with classmates, but rather an internal motivation to compete with myself to do my very best. They were not okay with me being average. As a result, I was referred and selected to be part of the gifted education program in elementary school and excelled in my studies. As I worked my way through elementary, middle school, and high school, I worked hard to get the best grades that I could. This meant staying up late to do homework and attempting to really understand what I was learning. These days I think people would say I enjoyed "doing the most."

I grew up in a diverse community in the southwest part of Houston, Texas. More specifically I grew up in Alief (*dubs up, neva down*), a community in southwest Houston known for its ethnic diversity. Growing up, I was surrounded by individuals from different cultures and backgrounds. I honestly thought most places looked like Alief. My next-door neighbor to the left was Mexican, my next-door neighbor to the right was Black, my neighbor across the street was Arab, my neighbor to the left of them was white, and my neighbor to the right of them was Vietnamese. Again, growing up I never thought of this as something unique, I simply thought this was what most of the United States was like. In school, I did learn that the United States was a melting pot, and as a first-generation Nigerian American, therefore, that rang true. It was not until my adolescence, when I got involved in sports and extracurricular activities, that I realized that some school districts we played against were not as diverse, but I do not think I gave it much thought looking back, I just chalked it up to an anomaly.

Socialization Experiences. As with most racial and ethnic minority parents in the United States, my parents prepared me for the realities of racism and discrimination in our society. They engaged in culturally-specific parenting practices, such as racial socialization, which includes teaching messages about racial and individual pride, preparation for bias, and intergroup relations among different racial groups (Coard & Sellers,

2005; Hughes et al., 2006; Stevenson, 1997). Growing up as a first-generation American, I received common preparation for biased messages such as, "you have to work twice as hard for half as much," but I also received additional messages such as, "obtaining a good education would allow me to be in charge of my future." From their perspective, being that I was born in the United States and did not have a pronounced accent, I would not be shut out of as many opportunities as they were. I guess they were partially right, my education has created significant access to opportunities I likely would not have otherwise, but it certainly has not been a magic pill to avoid gender discrimination and racism.

Despite growing up in a diverse community and attending a diverse school, Black girls were not expected to be smart, or often recognized for their intelligence. As is the case in many schools, the diversity represented in our students was not reflected by the teachers (Ford, 1998). In addition, the model minority myth meant that many of my classmates of Asian American backgrounds were held to much higher standards, while my achievements were often overlooked or downplayed. What confused me the most about this was that my peers could turn in cookie-cutter projects that they had copied from the internet, and their work would be applauded, while my objectively more creative and labor-intensive projects were seen as just okay. Almost with no regard to the difficulty or complexity of my work, it felt like I was graded on my skin color, and that meant that me, as a young Black girl, could never do something worthy of being regarded at the top. Despite this, I worked hard and continued to exceed personal goals I had set forth for myself. My parents and other Black or immigrant teachers expressed high expectations for me, and this too helped fuel me. I studied tirelessly in high school, participated in all the extracurriculars, and was the editor of my high school newspaper. I knew that I needed to get a scholarship to pay for college, and I could not let my parents, who had sacrificed so much for me down because I did not face my studies. In my senior year of high school, I was accepted into Northwestern University in Evanston IL, an elite private school that I knew very little about. Nevertheless, my parents, my father especially, were extremely excited, as was my high school counselor, a Black woman who eagerly encouraged me and wrote an insane amount of recommendation letters on my behalf during my senior year.

As I mentioned earlier, Black students at my school were rarely expected to excel academically and even when they were it was considered an anomaly rather than something to be expected. I'll spare you all the full story of having to prove my college acceptance by bringing my admission letter with me to class, despite spending the majority of high school ranking in the top 10 of my class. Again as a Black girl, it was beyond conceptualization that I was smart enough or had worked hard enough to get in, but rather it was another story that I think has particular context for this chapter. After mentioning that I was going to Northwestern, a classmate asked me, "How come Black people don't value education?" I responded with, "That's not true, I'm going to college and my parents would kill me if I told them I wasn't." He was quick to say, "But you're not Black, you're African. I mean like regular Black people." I countered him again, noting that my two best friends were "regular Black" by his definition, and they were also attending college, but clearly to him, that was an exception.

I remember going home that evening and recounting the experience to my father. He got very upset, and I was intrigued. He was adamant that what my peer had said was not only offensive, but also inaccurate. My father asked me where I thought "regular Black people" came from, and then mentioned that *even though we may have grown up and had different experiences, we were one*. He stated that to the broader society we would be looked at the same. He also recounted the discrimination that he experienced when first moving to the United States, alongside "regular Black" people, and noted how the discrimination and racism he witnessed and experienced was so horrible and shocking to him as an immigrant. At the end of the conversation, he instructed me that if anyone was to ever say that again in my presence, that I should shut the conversation down quickly, and highlight that we are all one and that we all similarly respect and value educational experiences. He also noted that education was about opportunity, and that not everyone has the opportunity to pursue education in the ways that they desire. He recounted to me how he always wanted to be a doctor, and how from a young age he thought he would be, until the science teacher at his school fell ill. They had a series of substitute teachers who weren't able to prepare them for the necessary science exams that were required for him to continue toward his desired path of becoming a doctor. Through no fault of his own, his dream was derailed, and he was forced to pursue educational opportunities that were available to him to ensure that he could move forward in his educational trajectory and get a job when he graduated. As he recounted the story, it was again another reminder that the illusion that everyone has equal access to opportunities was just that, an illusion. It was a moment that stuck with me. Still, it was not until later, in college, that I realized my trajectory (i.e., gifted and talented program, pre-AP, and AP classes, college) all came down to a single opportunity to get tested for the gifted and talented program, which ultimately led to me being tracked into the college preparatory courses. These opportunities that started in elementary school supported the values and educational goals my parents had for me as well.

Face Your Studies: Navigating the Nuance of "Opportunity"

Throughout high school, I worked hard to ensure that I would be able to apply for as many scholarships as possible to help pay for college. When it came time to apply for scholarships, I treated it like a job. I would go to school, come home and change, and go to my part-time job, and on days I didn't, I would come home and work on scholarship essays until I went to bed. My mom often sat on the couch alongside me, proofreading my essays. Fortunately, this paid off and I was the recipient of the Gates Millennium Scholarship, which provided significant financial support for me to attend college. The scholarship paid for everything above my family's expected contribution, as determined by the Free Application for Federal Student Aid, including student loans, work-study, etc. Despite this, there were still additional expenses, particularly associated with attending college out of state, and as a result, my father got a second full-time job overnight to help pay for these expenses. Although I was the one attending college, my parents very clearly showed me that they were there to support me in whatever way they could. In my head, I knew I could not squander the opportunity that they had provided for me.

Navigating college was challenging. I came from a working-class background and was suddenly surrounded by individuals whose parents made more money than I thought was possible, perhaps unless you were a celebrity. As I entered new spaces on campus, I was always followed by questions that seemed so out of place to me. One question I remember fondly was, "What does your father do?" It was so strange to me, why did everyone feel the need to ask me this? Being raised in a working-class community, jobs were jobs, they were a means to support yourself and your family. They often spoke very little about your identity, as they were so dependent on opportunity, and most individuals from my community seized whatever opportunity they could to provide for their families. This question was one of many reminders that my experiences were different from my peers.

My time at Northwestern was transformative for many reasons. I was forced to grow up with no family nearby, assimilate to a very new peer group, reconcile with persistent discriminatory experiences, and navigate a rigorous academic environment. College proved to be quite challenging in many ways. Again, I was met with experiences which confirmed that despite what I managed to achieve or do, these accomplishments would not be recognized in the same way as my peers. I remember one day near the end of the course, one of my professors went around and asked every student in the class what their future plans were. I was a Human Development and Psychological Services major, and the course was required. As we went around the classroom, an overwhelming majority of my classmates stated that they wanted to pursue Ph.D.s in Clinical Psychology. When it came time for my turn, as many had done before me, I proudly stated that I wanted to pursue a Ph.D. in Clinical Psychology. Unlike her enthusiastic response to everyone else, she scrunched her eyebrows in surprise and said "interesting," as she laughed. An overwhelming feeling of embarrassment came across me, and as I looked around almost to confirm that this had really happened, my fellow students quickly averted their gaze to avoid mine. Even as we walked out of the classroom, she stood at the door and as I walked past her, she pulled me to the side and questioned why I wanted to be a Clinical Psychologist. She went on to say that people like me would make good social workers and that a Ph.D. is really hard and difficult to get, so she didn't think it would be a good fit for me. Her voice was loud, and here she was once again embarrassing me in front of my peers, and telling me I wasn't good enough. I had an A in her class, nothing to suggest that I couldn't do "hard" things. She also had a blind grading system which she said helped eliminate bias. A large part of me wondered if that was something she had been forced to do, because she was clearly one of those people who failed at curbing her biases and racism.

This professor continued to make racist comments throughout the course, often staring at me as she made the comments. I wondered if she was daring me to challenge her, or if she wanted to see the offensiveness on my face. I managed by completely ignoring her presence in most classes and just doing my work. Northwestern was also the first time I was called the N-word to my face. I would often call my dad as he worked nights and tell him how hard things were for me at Northwestern, he would always respond with "Don't worry, just face your studies, and ignore the noise." The noise being anything bringing me down. Over time, "face your studies" had shifted to a phrase that encouraged me to persist, despite obstacles and a reminder to maximize all opportunities I had been afforded. Even if I didn't always see it, my father knew that on the other side of this struggle, there would be something worth it, so I followed his advice, working day and night and taking advantage of the opportunity to attend an elite private school and focus on school as my dad worked a second job to support me. Nevertheless, Northwestern was a place that afforded me many opportunities; when I mentioned to people that I went to Northwestern, they often remarked about how good of a school it was and often called me smart. Northwestern exposed me to careers and parts of academia I never knew existed. During my time at Northwestern, I grew a lot as an individual and again was presented with opportunities that I took advantage of to continue the pursuit of my personal and educational goals.

Face Your Studies: Building in and with Community

Following Northwestern, I pursued a Ph.D. in Clinical Psychology, but I did not go straight into a Ph.D. program. Given that I needed more research experience, I took a job at an academic medical center, building research skills to be competitive. While working there, at the urging of my mentor and my father, I pursued a pre-med post-bac. I worked full-time in downtown Chicago, and took the train over an hour to Evanston to take classes in the evening. The days were long and exhausting. I did my homework on my lunch break, going to the local McDonald's to get WI-FI, and completed it on other parts on the train ride. I was so exhausted and had such conflicting feelings about what I was doing. One day I decided to check-in to a hotel and spend the weekend figuring out my life. When I left, I decided to quit my post-bac program. My mom was excited and encouraging, my dad was encouraging too, but less excited. I think by dropping out of school he assumed that was it for me. We talked often and he never failed to remind me to "face my studies."

From this post-bac experience, I entered into a doctoral program. As with many clinical psychology doctoral programs, it contained a small cohort of students who went to school and took coursework together, that is, until we diverged into our own specialty research area. By nature, the program was designed to foster close relationships among members of the cohort. While I was used to being in spaces in which I was the only racial or ethnic minority, it felt different when we are all going through arguably one of the most challenging academic experiences of our lives, without seeing many people who looked like me. Even more challenging was the fact that many of the difficulties I faced in graduate school were directly tied to being a racial and ethnic minority in the program. Micro and macro aggressions became expected, rather than shocking.

In my first year, I joined an organization for minoritized graduate students. While I met people here and there and attended activities in my first year, I was not very active in the group. In my mind, it was still an extracurricular activity and I had to "face my studies" (*Naija voice*) first, as my father would always say. However, I soon came to realize that facing my studies also meant finding a supportive community within my academic home, that would also help me "face my studies." This realization was consistent with existing literature which states that social support is essential to student retention on higher-ed campuses (Wilcox et al., 2005). This organization provided a community. It was a space where I could be myself and exist with people who not only understood, but shared in many aspects of my doctoral experience.

Due to our shared background as minoritized students, they just got it. This group would also serve as an external fact check. The microaggressions from peers and faculty, the perceptions of their weakness or lack of intelligence were all echoed. We were all having the same experience, despite the fact that we were scattered in programs throughout the university with no connections to one another. Clearly, this was not an individual thing, rather a reminder that systemic racism and discrimination were ever present and would continue to be present throughout the doctoral experience. It proved to be such a re-affirming and validating experience, particularly as it relates to gaslighting, a discriminatory practice and term I had no clue existed until graduate school. As mentioned, this group allowed me to meet individuals who were not only similarly navigating a rigorous academic experience, but who also shared similar characteristics that would provide respite from the experiences in my doctoral program. And as you've read from the other women in this book, there were a subset of us, Black women, pursuing doctoral degrees who would come to rely on one another. We were a fierce source of support for one another. Without these women, I cannot fathom how I would have completed my degree. We would laugh together, cry together over collective traumatic experiences, and support one another as we often were very familiar with the challenges that each other faced in our doctoral programs.

Social support is often cited as a protective factor against a host of difficulties including, behavioral and mental health (Uchino et al., 1996; Uchino et al., 2018) and educational performance (Wilcox et al., 2005; Mishra, 2020). Thus, as I reflect on the support that this community of Black women doctoral students provided me, it is easy to see how our times with one another not only protected my mental health, but also contributed to the successful completion of my degree program. I could go on for days about the varying ways that these women supported me. From assisting me when I had my first tire blowout, serving as surrogate advisors and major professors, to bringing food and medication when I was sick, and keeping an eye on me during particularly low periods of my doctoral journey, when I didn't leave the couch. We supported each other through the difficult parts of the doctoral journey, but also celebrated and relished in each other's company during the more enjoyable times: workout buddies, dinner dates, road trip partners, hiking buddies, moving hands, and our Thursday-night Shondaland gatherings where we watched *Grey's Anatomy* and *How to Get Away with Murder*. These activities do not even begin to touch the surface of the activities shared together. I even remember one year, the same year I spent an extended period on my couch, I decided to redo my birthday. Birthdays had always been special to me growing up, I didn't usually have a big party, but every birthday spent with my family we had Domino's pizza and cake. It was my family's special way of celebrating one another's birthdays, as we seldom ordered pizza for any other occasion, a moment for us to all sit around and be together. Thus, I have always enjoyed birthday celebrations no matter how big or small. However, this particular year was a rough one and I didn't quite feel like celebrating. However, my friends, knowing that I always enjoyed forcing them to celebrate their own birthdays, forced me to celebrate mine. I reluctantly agreed to go to brunch with my group of girlfriends, but it was a blur, and I wasn't really in the mood to celebrate. After a failed comprehensive exam and barely passing my master's thesis, despite an entire summer spent at either school or the local coffee shop, I was exhausted and felt completely alone on my doctoral journey. Months went by and through the support of my friends and family things were looking up, so I did what anyone would do and decided to re-celebrate my birthday. We went all out, these amazing women bought me gifts, decorated my apartment, bought cake and ice cream, and even went shopping with me for the perfect outfit to re-celebrate my birthday four months later. We were sisters supporting each other no matter what wild idea we each had, such as celebrating a birthday redo. These women were part of the foundation of my doctoral experience, the *community* that helped me face my studies.

If these women were half of my foundation, my family was the other half. As I mentioned above, many of the challenges I faced in my doctoral studies were not unique to me, my friends, with whom we often sought solace with one another, dealt with their own challenges as well. Thus, the dual support of my community and close-knit family is what allowed me to achieve success in academia. As a doctoral student, I hung closely to my collectivist culture, which promoted the idea of collective support for achieving my goals. When I think of the ways in which my immigrant background influenced me the most through my doctoral studies, it was in emphasis on family, and by family, I mean nuclear family, but also my extended family as well. When my father first came to the United States, he came to join his siblings who had already immigrated. When I look at pictures of my parents when they were much younger, they are surrounded by family. We were a close-knit family, and this did not change when I went to college, nor when I went away again for graduate school, despite our distance. I spoke to my family daily, my mom was always good for a care package when I was sick or stressed or for holidays, such as Valentine's Day. I spoke to my aunt, my mom's older sibling weekly, even though she lived in Nigeria. She never failed to pray for me and wish me luck before an important exam, despite an 8-hour time difference. I remember fondly when I would struggle or get down on myself about a grade my dad would say to me it was "okay" and that "there will be more assignments." He would say to me with so much power in his voice, "*You don't really think the people in your class are smarter than you, you are smarter than all of them.*" He would tell me with so much conviction that "I was the smartest person in my class." Even if I didn't initially believe him, the conviction with which he repeated this to me over the years inspired me to always remain motivated, even in the face of challenges or defeat. When I would hit a wall, he often repeated this to me over the phone and it helped me continue to push forward.

While drawing on the support of my family came easy to me, at times it was in direct conflict with American societal expectations that proper development was meant to teach and promote independence. So much so that cultural values such as remaining at home with your family until marriage or until one feels ready to live independently were shunned. Even notions that I was speaking to family members daily were met with disapproving or negative comments suggesting I was enmeshed with my family. Regardless, I took great pride in my family's support for each other including, every WhatsApp video call to wish me luck prior to every academic milestone, morning messages of encouragement and prayers for my continued success, and congratulatory Facebook posts or messages celebrating successes with me. So, in those moments of isolation, or when the doctoral program was starting to get the best of me, I remembered that I had the support of my family members, near and far, rooting for me to succeed.

Conclusion

I learned many things throughout my doctoral studies, such as how to develop and hone critical thinking skills and how to write academic papers through the scientific process, but perhaps the most important thing I learned was that despite whatever lies ahead, I will always have the support of my family and friends. While I was in graduate school, I had a dry-erase board in my room complete with words of affirmation from my family and friends. They were written directly as told to me, in the voices of my family and friends. I saw them every night I went to bed and every morning when I woke up. When I was away from my apartment and found myself down or anxious, I would envision the board, and all the names on it that were supporting and encouraging me, and I would forge ahead.

I once had an older colleague ask, "Where can I find more 'smart' African Americans like you, and Keith (a pseudonym for the other Black person in my training program)?" Besides my initial shock at the question and a very long internal eye roll, I knew that the label of smart was only being affixed due to the need to identify diverse scholars for the colleague's proposed grant. Otherwise, she wouldn't have given a second thought to looking for minoritized scholars. In fact, in my work with her, it was obvious that she felt Black trainees were not as smart. I simply responded that "they are all over." Refusing to engage in the back and forth that I knew would ensue, which would again serve as a reminder that I was never expected to do well in that space, and that my worth as a scholar was only as important as it was to that individual's personal goals. I end on this note, not to say that the road to being where I am today is easy, but simply to say that there are amazingly talented Black women scholars and Black immigrant women scholars around us. While a pervasive lack of opportunity and formidable roadblocks makes it so that the road is paved with inequity and hardship, there are still many who persevere. So, if you find yourself asking this question, I implore you to look around at all the talented scholars around you that you have overlooked and undervalued. Finally, I ask that you "lift as you climb." I still don't remember exactly who gave me this advice or rather the words for this very important practice, but it serves as a great reminder for me to remember the importance of community, mentorship, and putting others in a position to do well. It also serves as an indirect reminder that we are inherently the product of our opportunities and thus, it is important to foster and create those for others as best as we can.

Acknowledgments. I am grateful to the editors for the invitation to be a part of this collective of immensely talented scholars. I want to dedicate this chapter to my parents, Toyin and Iyiola Are, my sister scholars, and my amazingly supportive family and friends.

References

Coard, S. I., & Sellers, R. M. (2005). African American families as a context for racial socialization. *African American family life: Ecological and cultural diversity*, 264–284.

Ford, D. Y. (1998). The underrepresentation of minority students in gifted education: Problems and promises in recruitment and retention. *The Journal of Special Education*, 32(1), 4–14.

Hughes, D., Bachman, M. A., Ruble, D. N., & Fuligni, A. (2006). Tuned In or Tuned Out: Parents' and Children's Interpretation of Parental Racial/Ethnic Socialization Practices. In L. Balter & C. S. Tamis-LeMonda (Eds.), *Child psychology: A handbook of contemporary issues* (pp. 591–610). Psychology Press.

Owens, J., & Lynch, S. M. (2012). Black and Hispanic immigrants' resilience against negative-ability racial stereotypes at selective colleges and universities in the United States. *Sociology of Education*, 85(4), 303–325. https://doi.org/10.1177/0038040711435856

Mishra, S. (2020). Social networks, social capital, social support and academic success in higher education: A systematic review with a special focus on 'underrepresented'students. *Educational Research Review, 29*, 100307.

Stevenson, H. C. (1997). Managing anger: Protective, proactive, or adaptive racial socialization identity profiles and African-American manhood development. *Journal of Prevention & Intervention in the Community, 16*, 35e61. http://dx.doi.org/10.1300/J005v16n01_03.

Uchino, B. N., Cacioppo, J. T., & Kiecolt-Glaser, J. K. (1996). The relationship between social support and physiological processes: A review with emphasis on underlying mechanisms and implications for health. *Psychological Bulletin, 119*(3), 488.

Uchino, B. N., Bowen, K., Kent de Grey, R., Mikel, J., & Fisher, E. B. (2018). Social support and physical health: Models, mechanisms, and opportunities. *Principles and concepts of behavioral medicine: A global handbook*, 341–372.

U.S. Census Bureau. (2017). Population Estimates, Ju U.S. Census Bureau (2021). Frequently Asked Questions (FAQs) About Foreign Born. Retrieved December 16, 2021, from https://www.census.gov/topics/population/foreign-born/about/faq.html#:~:text=The%20first%20generation%20refers%20to,with%20two%20U.S.%20native%20parents

Wilcox, P., Winn, S., & Fyvie-Gauld, M. (2005). 'It was nothing to do with the university, it was just the people': The role of social support in the first-year experience of higher education. *Studies in Higher Education, 30*(6), 707–722.

5
THE EVOLUTION OF MY BIRACIAL IDENTITY THROUGH ATTENDING TWO PREDOMINATELY WHITE INSTITUTIONS

Megan Hicks, Ph.D.

> *I have to admit it, there are many times in my life where I have to shut one part of myself off to the world.*

This chapter focuses on my experience of being a Biracial woman navigating the doctoral process in a community with other Black women, a sense of group membership, as well as the experience of identifying as Black, while familial support was primarily white. I think it is important for me to start with a discussion about my racial identity and my journey to identifying myself as a Black-identifying Biracial woman. Then, I will unpack how my journey, with an emphasis on my racial and academic identity, and how this shaped my experience attending a predominantly white institution (PWI) while earning my doctoral degree.

Racial Identity Development from Elementary Through High School

Limited scholarship focuses on the experiences of Biracial experiences in gifted programs, and most of the relevant research centers on racial identity, self-concept/esteem, and microaggressions (Ford et al., 2016; Baxley, 2008; Pople, 2015). There is a missing lens in respect to the racialized gendered experiences of Biracial individuals, and the ways in which they navigate programs, family dynamics, and the bilateral lens in which they see the world. My narrative aims to provide a scope to understand the endarkened experiences of my racial landscape and academic identity, particularly as I unpack otherness (Zevallos, 2013).

DOI: 10.4324/9781003292180-6

My racial identity has evolved many times throughout my life. As I reflect on the different stages of my life, there was much confusion about my racial identity starting at a very young age. As we know, place matters, and I grew up in a rural county in Ohio, where I was one of two Black-identifying people in my senior class. For most of my formative years, I was the only Black person in my school for most of my life. Additionally, my mother and my family are white, excluding my Biracial younger brother. During my formative years, I did not and still do not have a relationship with my father's family. Therefore, when I talk about my family in this chapter, it will be in reference to my white family. Although my mother functioned as a single mother, I was primarily raised by my grandparents, but bounced back and forth between them and my mother's house. She was very independent and determined in her life; she was a Marine and a factory worker. I tell myself that I got my strong independence and determination from her.

As previously mentioned, there was much confusion growing up. During my elementary school years, I identified as white, because this is all that I knew. My family was white, my friends were white, my teachers were white, and all of my toys were white. In elementary school, I think there was a lot of pressure from educators and family members to make me feel that I was no different from anyone else. Therefore, they just tried to merge me into the current social climate, which meant that I was socialized to be white.

Being socialized as white, my community and friends were homogenous; mostly identifying as white, rural, and low-middle income. I was from a very small farm town where multiple family generations grew up and grew old. Very few people left. I was the first person in my family to get a graduate-level degree. Throughout elementary and middle school, I grew more confused about why my skin looked different, because that was the only difference that I felt at the time. My Memaw has told me that I tried to scrub my skin off in the bathtub, asking her why it was dirty. My Memaw replied, "Your skin is not dirty. God just left you in the oven a little longer, that's all." These small moments with Memaw always stuck with me throughout the different stages of my identity. Memaw did try hard to make me feel loved and included. However, as I grew and became more aware of the world, I learned that I did not receive any racial socialization from my family at all. Feeling like an outsider became clearer as I grew older.

Racial discrimination significantly increased as I entered my high school years. I was called a ni**er multiple times, received death threats, and someone threatened to cut my brake lines. I was spit on. Socially, I never dated anyone. These racist acts really took a toll on my view of the world and my mental health. These acts made me feel isolated and depressed. During this time, I started to harm myself and experimented with substances. Additionally, in my eyes, my family did not see how these racially motivated acts were racist. My family had an overall lack of awareness, and this caused me to socially isolate myself within my family. However, a few good things did come out of my high school years.

It was in high school that I discovered how gifted I was academically. Because of where my school was situated, my high school only offered one AP class, and I took it. It was here I began to lean into course/subject area content and found varying levels of intrinsic motivation to achieve. I was in the National Honor Society, a society for academic excellence. It was here I began to create a new narrative for myself around my sense of liberation; I would use academics to take me to places away from this small town in Ohio.

Navigating Gifted Spaces with a Confusing Biracial Identity

Even though I was gifted academically, my brown skin still imposed stereotypes on me that impacted my mental health, worldview, and academic dexterity. I remember one student saying to me, "Wow, I didn't know that you were smart enough to be in the National Honor Society." I noticed early on, that with my accomplishments, everyone was always shocked rather than expecting when I would accomplish anything in school. My achievements at school were founded in surprise, followed by a dismissal. People in my school and in my community often made comments about how there had to be other reasons why I was accomplishing great things academically, because "I was Black." These negative comments impacted my sense of self-worth and esteem; consequently leaving me feeling low. However, I was still determined to get out of the small town where I could feel that my giftedness and Blackness were appreciated.

Finding a Place to Belong at My First Predominately White Undergraduate Institution

Racial discrimination, feelings of isolation, and depression were the main motivators for applying to a large university. One university that was recruiting heavily in my area was The Ohio State University (OSU). I would receive their brochures and they made the campus look so diverse. I even received an invitation from the Multicultural Student Office to attend a basketball game at OSU for prospective students. My mother drove me three hours to OSU to experience the game. The basketball game was life-changing for me; I got to meet many different students from varying backgrounds who also received an invitation. I made the decision that evening that I wanted to go to OSU after high school.

OSU seemed like a great start for me, with regard to my academics and my racial identity journey. Based on the experiences in my hometown and the visceral feelings associated with this space, I wanted to go to college far away from home to pull me out of my comfort zone. For my college experience, I wanted a diverse space so that I could learn more about different cultures and find my community of people. It was the happiest day of my life when I was accepted with a full tuition scholarship. From the first day that I received my acceptance letter, I dreamt of everything that I would do once I got to campus.

It's the Community for Me!

From the moment I arrived on campus, I went into full exploration mode. I was stepping into a newfound identity that I created, without influence from my family or my hometown. I attended all of the cultural events and festivals the University had to offer. I enrolled in multiple African American history classes and engaged in the Black Student Association. I developed a great group of friends, several gifted Black and Biracial women. This was also the first time in my life that I was surrounded by a community of gifted Black women. Incredibly motivating! They were in school to become doctors, lawyers, chemists, biologists, lawyers, psychologists, business women, and the list could go on and on.

Meeting these women made me feel alive for the first time in my life! I always joke that I received my Black racial socialization from them, but this concept holds to be true. These gifted Black women taught me how to take care of my hair and my skin. They made me mixtapes of popular music, and they explained social norms to me that I did not understand. They taught me what it meant to support one another fully and unconditionally. It was at this time that I decided to identify as strictly Black. I was overcome with a sense of cultural pride. The Black women that I connected with allowed me to understand the meaning of Black excellence.

However, this heightened sense of cultural pride did not come without its own challenges. As I learned more about my life and my Black culture, it sparked more questions about who I was inside of me. I became extremely exhausted with explaining myself, and where I came from to others. I was a Black girl who was raised in a rural county in Ohio with a white family, and my white side did not have a sense of cultural pride. I vacillated back to low self-esteem and questioned who I was. Luckily, I was surrounded by an amazing group of women who supported me and helped me process these emotions. They taught me that I just needed to be myself. They accepted me for the different person that I was and showed me that Black women are not a monolith. We possess our own unique qualities and personalities that make us great. As graduation day came and went I am still as close with these women as the day we met in 2007. I will always be grateful for the relationships of these women and how they shaped me into the person I am today. They served as motivation for me to always push to be the best version of myself and they are the main reason that I applied to graduate school.

Finding Black Girl Magic at My Predominately White Graduate Institution

Destined for greatness, I applied to one graduate school in 2011. I wanted to be near my family in the South, and this particular PWI had a pipeline to a graduate school program. This bridge program to graduate school was for Black students and provided resources on how to get there. At the time, I was the first person in my family to go to graduate school. I thought that I did not possess the skills nor have the support to successfully apply and get into it, and this pathway program was a great resource for me. I was accepted into the pathway program and received an invitation for a campus visit. A major component of this visit was to interview in the department that you will be applying to enter. I remember arriving on campus and immediately feeling like a fish out of water. The South and the campus were just very different from everything I'd ever known. Even though I was not a stranger to academically white spaces, this space just felt heavier.

A significant event happened during my campus interview with my future department. I remember expressing general concerns to the graduate coordinator about the program, and I received the reply of, "Possibly this space isn't for you." She made me feel that if I could not assimilate to this space, then it would be better for me to just not be there. I felt discouraged leaving that meeting. I remember processing with my friends after that, and one friend said, "Of course she said that. We know this space wasn't created for us." However, I could see myself creating positive change in that department, and my mind was determined to work with a specific person in a specific research center at that university.

I finished the pathway program and turned in my application to this program. I did not expect to get in after that horrible interview. However, I received my decision letter in the mail, and to my surprise, was admitted and received a graduate assistantship to pay for my education. I accepted and planned to attend that fall. Once the fall came, I was so nervous. I arrived late to orientation and felt that I was not starting on the best foundation. I had a spiral of emotions. The interview with the graduate coordinator played repeatedly in my head. Had I made a huge mistake? Was this space really not for me? I received my flight information and was told by my department there was another woman attending the orientation late. We would ride together to orientation. This gave me slight comfort.

I remember sitting at the airport waiting for ground transportation playing the questions over again in my head. Had I made a huge mistake? Was this space really not for me? I remember looking up, and there was this Black woman in a blue blazer waiting for the same shuttle as I was. This was the moment that I made my first graduate school bestie, a fellow gifted Black woman. The shuttle arrived, and we started talking to each other. I remember feeling, "Maybe this will be alright." We arrived at our orientation and then went on to the university-wide graduate school orientation. There were so many people. I had these same feelings rush over me again. Did I make a huge mistake coming here?

Then, I saw a beautiful Black woman stand up on stage at orientation in front of thousands of people to give an official welcome. She was the president of a Graduate and Professional Scholars (GAPS) organization. Her speech made me feel welcome again. It gave me a reminder that even though there were only a few Black/Brown faces in the crowd at the orientation, this was our space too. After orientation, there was an involvement fair. I saw the table for this GAPS organization. Before I could walk up to the table, I heard a woman say in a prominent voice, "Hello there! Are you interested in GAPS?" It was her. I had a huge smile on my face, she greeted me with such warmth. She and I spoke for a while, and we found out that we had gone to the same undergraduate school in Ohio. That connection with her really meant a lot to me, and she is an amazing friend and mentor to this day.

Meeting two gifted Black women on the same day of my first week of graduate school is instilled in my heart forever, and I replay it whenever I have my doubts or had doubts about graduate school. It served as a reminder that I have a supportive network that is there for me every day and genuinely wants me to succeed, as I do for them.

Navigating the Doctoral Experience of Being Biracial at a PWI

My doctoral experience can be summed up by a quote from Patricia Hill Collins:

> Theory of all types is often presented as being so abstract that it can be appreciated only by a select few. Though often highly satisfying to

academics, this definition excludes those who do not speak the language of elites and thus reinforces social relations of domination. Educated elites typically claim that only they are qualified to produce theory and believe that only they can interpret not only their own but everyone else's experiences. Moreover, educated elites often use this belief to uphold their own privilege.

(2002, p. vii)

Beginning graduate school as a Biracial woman at a PWI in the South was a difficult task. My perspective and lived experiences caused conflicts among my advising committee. Even in the classroom, I would learn a concept, and I could not relate to the concept because my lived experience taught me otherwise. I would challenge these concepts and theoretical frameworks. I noticed when I challenged these ways of thinking, I was met with hostility followed by imposed stereotyping and a questioning of my intelligence. It was clear that my professors thought that I could never become one of the "educated elite."

A memory that I will always carry with me was my qualifying comprehensive exams. I was questioned by a committee of three white men about the experiences of Black youth. They were saying how previous research and theory did not exactly align with my proposed hypotheses. I remember saying, "Well, through lived experience, this is how I interpret these associations." We had a long conversation back and forth about how previous research and theory have not established that in the current field of knowledge. I stood strong to my truth. I passed my exams, but it was not without contest.

Questioning My Identity...Again

As I entered graduate school in full swing, I grew close with my cohort and met more amazing and supportive classmates. I joined GAPS and broadened my supportive network. It was such a pleasure to meet Black and Brown scholars across all programs and from all walks of life, in different seasons of their life. I am so blessed to have made these connections and to have made them at such a perfect time. I had no idea what turn of events would happen during that time in my program, but these connections I made were crucial.

It was during my first year of graduate school in Spring 2012 that Trayvon Martin was murdered. Being Biracial during this time was very difficult. I experienced contention in my family, in the world, and at school. My family did not know how to support me, and I perceived them as not trying to support me during this time. I remember hearing the news of Trayvon Martin, and I watched and listened as my friends called their families to process. My family, at the time, did not have the racial and social awareness that they do now. Race was not something we talked about. I had never spoken to my family in my adult years of life about how race impacted my life, and I perceived them as not caring to even ask.

Trayvon's murder sparked this questioning of my racial identity again and made me question if I could complete my graduate degree. Many conversations surrounding race happened during the time of Trayvon's case, and I felt that I was not educated enough to advocate for the Black community in this time of need. In addition to feeling not educated enough, I was having difficult conversations with my family. I felt unheard and unsupported. However, I discovered that I did have an outlet to process the pain. I had my cohort of classmates, my GAPS family, and my group of gifted Black women. I would have not made it through without them. This network of people educated me on what was important. They provided a space for me to learn how to articulate myself on important issues and process how my Biracial identity is important. I learned that I could use my Biracial identity to bridge the gap between "Black and white." I learned that being Biracial allowed me to have a voice in a special place. In conversations about racial issues, I could bring in a perspective informed by growing up in a white and rural space but also understanding racial discrimination and having the Black lived experience. Having this Biracial experience started to empower me and I began to understand my importance in higher education. This fueled my fire to continue on in my doctoral degree program.

As I continued in my program with my regained Biracial identity, I thought it would be smooth sailing. I was working for my purpose. I became the Biracial scholar that I wanted to see in academia. I was proud of both sides of my identity. However, in 2014, this path changed forever. This was the brutal year that we lost Dontre Hamilton, Eric Gardner, John Crawford, Michael Brown, Tamir Rice, and many more to the brutality of the police. Shortly after this, we lost Sandra Bland, Walter Scott, Freddie Gray, and many others. Then, 2016 marked the beginning of the Donald Trump presidency.

To be truthful, during this time frame, there were moments when I did not want to be Biracial. I am not saying that I didn't want to be Black, or that I didn't want to be white. To have to navigate a middle ground again in spaces where you cannot be in the middle was the most difficult time in my life. I was grieving the loss of Black lives, while having racial battles within my own family. All these events sparked new conversations in my family that had never happened before. These events also required you to take a stand for justice or be tolerant in silence. I decided to take a stand for justice, and this created a division in my family that has not been completely repaired.

As I stood for justice, I felt completely isolated from my family, and this took a toll on my studies. I remember not being able to go to class or work for multiple days. Luckily, I had my community to help pull me out of the darkness. They educated me on actions I could do in the community to feel empowered. I participated in my first public protest. This was the most empowering feeling I have ever felt, to stand side by side with my tribe of Black women and fight for justice.

On the other hand of being Biracial, while feeling empowered to stand for justice and fight for the Black community, my white family interpreted these actions as standing up against them. I had family members who voted for Trump. This caused a strong division in my family. We were and still are faced with many tough conversations. This really impacted my journey in my doctoral program. Throughout my doctoral program process, we were and still are having tough conversations, yet remained close despite the contention. They provided me with important advice and information when I needed it. One time during my doctoral program, I received feedback from my advisor that I needed to have a presence in the classroom. They said that I needed to have a voice and articulate myself in a specific way. My advisor told me that they didn't think I could "make it in academia" if I didn't change how I presented myself. I was told I would not be able to teach classes or succeed at a research-one university. I understand now how racist that feedback was, but during that time, I leaned on my family. They showed me how to walk into rooms and command a presence. They taught me how to draft emails with specific language. They showed me how to operate in a very white male-dominated space and I appreciated them so much for helping me succeed in this way.

During 2016–2017, I developed a deep depression from having very close family members stand on the opposite side of important social issues as me. I felt very in the middle of a huge fight for justice. Do I stand up for justice and lose my family? Is it possible to keep both? Do I want to keep the relationships with the family that I have knowing what they stand for? Am I able to still do the work and advocate for the Black community, while also being Biracial? I learned that these questions are very hard to answer. I am not sure if we have fully figured it out. However, I do know what I stand for. I know the importance of my presence in certain rooms at specific tables. I know that I need to be a voice and provide a perspective that may not always be welcomed, but it is needed. I know there is a bigger purpose for a Biracial woman like me to earn a PhD. I had to be among the six percent of Black Ph.D.s. I had to complete my degree for the little gifted Biracial girls coming up after me.

Suggestions for Navigating a PWI as a Biracial Woman

As I close out this chapter, I wanted to provide suggestions for navigating a PWI as a Biracial woman. I hope these suggestions may be helpful in guiding you through the doctoral process.

Black Girl Magic. Throughout my narrative, I hope that I have shown the importance of being around a group of gifted Black women. I had the privilege of experiencing this many times throughout my life. I truly believe that I would have not made it through each phase of my life without each one of them. It is important to have people around you that fill each cup that you need to be filled. It is important to have diversity in your tribe so that you can receive feedback from different perspectives. It is important to have your work tribe, the group of friends who will be up at the library with you writing until 3 a.m. It is important to have your fun tribe, the group of friends that will pull up at your house and force you to come outside. They show you the importance of balance. It is important to have the tribe of women who have come before you. They can shine a light on your path in places that may seem extra dark. They can provide mentorship and provide guidance on how to navigate the doctoral process.

Embrace all sides of yourself and appreciate them as strengths. As a Biracial woman navigating a PWI, it was also helpful for me to receive advice from my white family who have experience communicating in formal spaces that I needed assistance with. I mentioned how my family helped me navigate the social norms that I did not know in academia. The social norms of how to communicate in meetings and in the academic setting were very unfamiliar to me. Also, my advisory committee consisted of three white men. It was tough to communicate in meetings and through email with my committee. I was raised to be seen and not heard when in rooms with people of authority. My department thought this was a negative thing and questioned my ability to lead a team or teach a course. My family members were pivotal in coaching me on how to communicate in these spaces and how to respond to specific situations to get across the points that I wanted to convey.

Stand in your truth. Another point that relates to my struggle with communication is that my identity confused people, especially my advisors. It was clear when my relationships began with them, they had certain biases and assumptions about how I should act, what I should know, and what accomplishments I would achieve. My perspective of thinking and lived experiences did not always match existing research or theory.

My research focused on community and contextual factors that influence health risk behaviors among Black families. Through lived experience, I had a different way of identifying risk and protective factors. My way of thinking was always questioned because it didn't align with the existing field of research.

To that, I say, *stand in your truth*. There were a few moments throughout my PhD where I stood in my truth, and it paid off immensely. I received awards, and I won competitions. My truth eventually became a staple in the current landscape of knowledge in my field. Do not let anyone make you second-guess your giftedness or your contributions to your work.

Communicate. Lastly, I think I should actually write *overcommunicate*. In your program, it is important to communicate your needs, unique perspectives, struggles, and successes. You never know what opportunities may arise for you or what hindrances may be spoken about you behind closed doors. It is important to advocate for yourself and communicate to reduce assumptions made about you. It is important to communicate with your friends and family. The doctoral process can be a lonely process. If you need to disappear and focus on your studies for a while, it is important to communicate with your loved ones about how they can support you. It is especially important to communicate with those not familiar with the doctoral process. I know this was very difficult for my family to understand. I had to overcommunicate about my workload, expectations, and how I was feeling to get them to understand the real commitment it takes to complete a doctoral degree.

Conclusion

As a Biracial woman who graduated from multiple PWIs, I have seen the importance of our presence in these spaces. Our perspective is needed there. It is needed to confuse people and to challenge them to think outside of the box. It may get frustrating to always have to explain yourself, but do not let this dim your light. I hope Biracial women can use those moments of frustration as beacons of light for growth, exploration, and understanding. I hope this chapter of my narrative may serve as a lighthouse for other Biracial gifted Black women attending PWIs to look to and assist in their own journey forward.

References

Baxley, T. P. (2008). "What are you?" Biracial children in the classroom. *Childhood Education*, 84(4), 230–233.

Collins, P. H. (2002). *Black feminist thought: Knowledge, consciousness, and the politics of empowerment*. Routledge Publishing.

Ford, D. Y., Whiting, G. W., & Goings, R. B. (2016). Biracial and multiracial gifted students: Looking for a grain of rice in a box of sand. In C. W. Lewis & J. L. Moore III *Gifted children of color around the world: Diverse needs, exemplary practices, and directions for the future* (Vol. 3, pp. 121–135). Emerald Group Publishing Limited.

Pople, C. E. (2015). *Gifted black and biracial students at a predominantly white gifted school* (Order No. 3712830). Available from ProQuest Central; ProQuest Dissertations & Theses Global; Social Science Premium Collection. (1707357450). https://www.proquest.com/dissertations-theses/gifted-black-biracial-students-at-predominantly/docview/1707357450/se-2

Zavellos, Z. (2013, January 9). *The other sociologist analysis of difference* [web log comment]. http://othersociologist.com/otherness-resources/

6

ALL OF ME

Centering *Homeplace* in Personal and Professional Reflections of Becoming a Blackgirl Motherscholar

Taryrn T.C. Brown, Ph.D.

The song, "To Zion" is a well-known emotional apex of the award-winning musical project, *The Miseducation of Lauryn Hill* (1998). This record was Hill's love letter to her firstborn, Zion David Marley, and was a project full of emotional turning points. As a musical representation of the unbridled joy only a mother can feel the first time she feels her child move in her womb, this song captures the very essence of what my lived experience has been in the grand gesturing towards my Blackgirl motherscholar identity, and what continues to be the impetus of my pursuits in academia. A gesture that, through this chapter, rests retrospectively in my six-year-long journey of being, embodying, and becoming all of me in pursuit of the Ph.D. "To Zion" is about the bond between a mother and her first child, but it's also about a woman's choice and connection to their mothering, their evolving homeplace- and their *voice*.

Introduction

Blackgirls face a variety of factors historical, institutional, and social- that heighten the weight and barriers they face as they move through spaces (Butler, 2018; Cahill, 2021). I use the term, Blackgirl (Boylorn, 2016; Hill, 2019) [one word] to capture the fluid negotiations of time and space for Black women that are not bound by fragmented narratives of racialized and gendered discourses. The term Blackgirl "rejects compartmentalizing Blackgirls' lives, stories, and bodies and serves as a symbolic transgression to see them/us as complex and whole" (Hill, 2019, p. 3). Centering historical, institutional, and social realities of Blackgirls allow our stories to manifest as funds of knowledge. Foregrounded in Black feminist/womanist scholarship (Dillard, 2000), this alternative approach to inquiry places emphasis on the multiple ways of knowing that Blackgirl epistemologies offer toward retrospective storytelling and Afro-Futuristic possibility. These opportunities also story-lived experiences, to allow intuition to serve as valid and privileged personal testimony and discourse. Collins (2000) states,

> Oppressed groups are frequently placed in the situation of being listened to only if we frame our ideas in the language that is familiar to and comfortable for a dominant group. This requirement often changes the meaning of our ideas and works to elevate the ideas of dominant groups.
>
> *(p. xiii)*

As an educator and scholar, I have always foregrounded my pedagogical philosophy in Black feminism and the power of voice. In this way, I have worked to challenge systems and barriers in an attempt to amplify minoritized identities beyond survivability toward a generative frame of belonging, community, justice, and equity. A growing confidence of belonging, that for me personally, was troubled throughout my doctoral journey, which was an anomaly from my earlier navigations of learning spaces as a gifted Blackgirl across educational contexts over the years. In merging the frameworks of Blackgirl autoethnography, motherwork, and motherscholarship, this chapter captures my *(re)memories* during my pursuit of the Ph.D., an experience that now frames my positionality within the academy and beyond.

Blackgirl Motherscholar Autoethnography

As coined by critical scholar Robin Boylorn, Blackgirl autoethnography emerges as a method for centering internal and external lived realities that resist stereotypical notions of Blackgirlhood even if/when the outside world attempts to silence Blackgirls (Boylorn, 2013). Utilizing Blackgirl autoethnography in this chapter, I define my emerging identity in what Matias (2011) titles a motherscholar framework, and within the spatiality of my *homeplace*. Motherscholars in the discipline of education assert that when motherhood and intellect confront and inform each other, a new thinking emerges to capture the possibility of humanizing education beyond the private relationships between mothers and children. These experiences more explicitly informed my navigation as a doctoral student, and even now as I complete my third year as faculty within the academy.

Motherscholarship centers the tensions that emerge from mothering discourses that suggest a singular mothering experience, void of nuances, explicitly at the intersection of mothering, academia, and the professoriate.

In offering a foundation for considerations of discourses on motherhood, Glenn et al. (1994) posit mothering as a stable, inviolable category, something which is self-evident, rather than an activity, which is informed by and reflects the socio-political pre-occupations of a particular time and place. Mothering, like most societal measures, is a socially constructed perspective that cannot continue to be analyzed in isolation. From a feminist perspective, gender roles are the product of local norms and social pressures (Durkin, 1995; hooks, 1994), with the idea of mothering playing a huge role in the perceptions and social pressures that shape many women's experiences (Glenn et al., 1994; Lapayese, 2012; Matias, 2011). With these implications in mind, motherscholaring creates space for considering the complexities of socialized negotiations of motherhood, toward an inclusion of factors such as individuality, social circumstance, financial position, and employment status that also shape lived experience in emerging mothering realities (Phoenix & Woolett, 1991).

For this chapter, a motherscholar framework also embraces Blackgirlness, as I respond and highlight moments that informed some of my academic milestones- graduate school, doctoral candidacy, dissertation defense, and the job search. Orienting my lived experiences across the methodological strengths of Blackgirl autoethnography, motherscholar framing, and drawing upon hooks (1994) and Collins's (2000) contributions to the subject of mothering and the home as *homeplace*, this chapter creates space for crafting a cultural lens by which I hope to contribute in Black women realities in pursuit of the Ph.D. and the embodied Black motherscholar identity.

(Re)membrances of Me Whole: Marriage, Motherwork, and Mattering

Blackgirls are not a monolith, so I am prompted to start my retrospection by centering who I am. Our names and identities are often descriptors of who we currently are, and hopefully who we aim to become. They can also be a present-day representation of how we perceive ourselves in this world or feel valued, affirmed, or welcomed in the spaces (Butler, 2018; Cahill, 2021) we navigate. For me, I've always been the little girl with the big Zimbabwean name; little Miss Taryrn Tinasha Chemwandoita Njagu, now Brown. A name that, in my reflections, took a while to learn to spell but was filled with histories and generations of family legacy and traditions. I am second generation Chemwanodoita, the namesake to my grandmother who was a domestic science educator that kept a home and family across international borders, as she traveled with my grandfather to the U.S. in the early 1960s. They journeyed all the way back home to the capital city of Harare, Zimbabwe where she would mother four children, the second eldest being my father. My name always was so meaningful, even before I truly realized its meaning; Chemwandoita, in the Shona language, means, "Anything you can do I can do better or one more." And that was a name that my mother, chest proud, would always affirm assuredly in my upbringing, and which has become a guide for me as I have navigated the uncertainties of life. Uncertainties that would take this Blackgirl with the big Zimbabwean name to places the generations before had worked so hard to lay precedence for.

Throughout my educational experiences, at both the elementary and secondary levels, I was known as the smart Black girl. Often one of two Black girls in the gifted program or within the Honors and Advanced Placement courses I would have in middle and high school, I can recall memories of correction, as I and the other Black girl were often correcting the teachers or peers who would interchange our names as if our likeness were one and the same. As a teenager, more directly, this aspect of my identity became further convoluted as I sought refuge through extracurricular involvement in more culturally diverse spaces, but would spend the majority of my day isolated from these communities in many of my classes. In retrospect, my experiences navigating these high-achieving academic spaces perpetuated a space of *othering* that would follow me throughout my academic journey.

Initially, I always thought I would be a medical doctor until the Summer of 2002, when I would participate in a high school residency mentoring program that would seal my disinterest in seeing people physically at their worst, and needing to not faint in the moment from the graphic realities of the emergency room. It was in my master's program, however, that I developed relationships with scholar-practitioners that were doing the work that I never considered a possibility for myself. Watching them center scholarship and practice that disrupted systems and structures which limited access for minoritized communities inspired me to consider possibilities in academia; even when I did not quite realize that was the case.

In retrospect, there were a myriad of experiences that have shaped these moments for me. Some of which until now, I have placed out of my purview because of the ripples of emotion that permeate from those spaces of remembrance. These moments are my first reconnections with my embodied *motherwork* (Collins, 1994), that was forming during this time. Collins (1994) introduces the term *motherwork* to break down the liberal dichotomies implicit in the experiences between the public and the private, community and individual. It seeks to centralize the concerns of women of color's priorities in ensuring *physical survival, empowerment*, and the maintenance of *cultural identity* in the face of racism. Dillard beautifully remarks,

> So how did we, as a Black people- the original people- learn to forget? Why does that forgetting matter? And how do we (re)member? It matters because, from the continent of Africa through her diaspora, we are one people. It matters because the strength of a people can be measured in how we take care of our babies and the women and elders among us. It matters because we are a people who have endured immeasurable suffering and still hung onto each other, and to others, and loved hard.
> *(2022, p. 6)*

As I began to consider how I wanted to organize my thoughts around my doctoral journey as a contributor to the broader discourse surrounding Black women's experiences in academia, I was reminded of various experiences that I had to neglect or put on the shelf at different points, to manage the other intersectional aspects of my identity. These memories now, however, frame key periods of time in my Ph.D. journey that continue to inform my pedagogies and praxis as a scholar-practitioner. The following sections will capture some of those key periods of experience, with rich examples of what it felt like in my pursuit of the Ph.D., and the backward and forward pushes throughout my journey to consider my own mattering in academia.

The Original Mixtape: Young Black Love, Established in 2012

My husband and I met at the American College Personnel Association Annual Conference in March of 2011. Both student affairs practitioners at the time, we had traveled to Baltimore for the conference to assist our respective institutions with staff hiring. As attendees at the evening's National Panhellenic Council social, our brief passing would lead to seven months of dating and then seven months of engagement. We married in the Summer of 2012, just a couple of months after finding out I had been admitted to the Social Foundations Ph.D. program at Southeastern University. I remember my first in-person visit with my advisor. The meeting came just a few short weeks after our small intimate wedding ceremony, which consisted of only our immediate family members and church clergy. With my eyes bright and eager to arrive on campus for my first advisory meeting with my assigned mentor, I remember walking hand-in-hand into the College of Education, ready to embark on what I didn't realize would be one of the hardest challenges in my educational life. My previous experiences in education had always come a little easy, having navigated advanced placements and honors learning spaces. This journey through the Ph.D., however, would trouble the gifted Blackgirl confidence that traveled with me into my first advisory meeting.

My husband had taken the day off to ride with me to the College for the meeting, as we lived in downtown Atlanta. I remember walking into my advisor's office all smiles, my husband a little behind me. I wanted to introduce him before he went off to wander campus for the duration of my meeting. My advisor at the time greeted us both and I walked nervously into her office for the meeting. Almost instantly, my advisor inquired into my relationship, as she asked, "So when did you get married?"

I remember excitedly responding as we were just a few weeks in, "Back in June! We are newlyweds."

Her facial response offered a mild smirk as she then stated, "Well you aren't planning on having kids soon, are you?" I remember at that moment, how quickly I responded, "Oh no!" We had already fielded similar sentiments from eager parents on both sides of our families about our intended timeline for kids.

She proceeded to share stories of experiences of past doctoral students she had mentored, who had not completed their doctorate because they had gotten married and had children. A warning she wanted to share with me, to take heed in advance of the start of my courses that would begin a few short weeks later.

This fleeting moment foreshadowed my journey- although I didn't realize it at the time. A moment that I would vividly remember when I would find out I was pregnant with my first child, and a moment that would shape the remaining years of my Ph.D. journey in a tremendous way.

The Remix: My First Born in 2014

I found out I was pregnant in my last semester of coursework for my Ph.D. in Social Foundations. I was thrilled! My husband and I had not really been planning to get pregnant so soon, but we are so thankful for the blessing that would be our first-born son. It was in that semester that I would meet a forever sister in my Ph.D. journey and my emerging sister-scholar network. We had taken a class together prior to that semester, but this was our first in-person course and probably the hardest class I had to take during my journey- Educational Statistics.

My first pregnancy seemed to give me academic superpowers- well at least I thought so. I was inspired, dedicated, motivated, and focused. I had the "glow" that many attributed to pregnancy, and would commute two-plus hours every day to take my courses and to work in my assistantship. This assistantship was in a community-embedded educational center that was run by another faculty mentor in the college. That glow and excitement, however, soon gave way to the realities of motherhood in academia. I remember the sheer dread I felt in sharing with my advisor that I was pregnant. What would she think? Would she expect my path in this space to now mirror the stories she had shared during my first campus visit? On the day of sharing the news with my advisor, I had emotionally prepared myself for the unknowns that had filled my thoughts in the weeks prior. With notes and strategy for how I had anticipated my continued matriculation through the program, I remember sharing my news over an afternoon lunch meeting. Immediately, I was prompted to consider my continued goals in the program. The excitement I had navigated in sharing this same news with so many others, however, in this moment, was met with further anxieties around whether or not my preparedness for the anticipated questions could truly be enough to maintain my tenacity in my doctoral program.

Conversations with other students who were not mothers themselves, also now focused on my pregnancy and how I was "handling everything," rather than on my research. Faculty members began offering unsolicited suggestions about alternative jobs for a Ph.D. beyond academia, a possibility that had never come up before I gave birth. Increasingly, I began realizing how cultural attitudes and institutional hurdles shift- making mothers feel unwelcome in the ivory tower. This experience was even more heightened for me, as the physicality of being pregnant drew additional attention as I maneuvered campus life.

These negotiations came to a tumultuous head, following a couple of years of toxic rhetoric around my inability to manage the expectations of mothering and home, alongside my doctoral studies. Years that shook the confidence and joy that I brought into the program and that had me questioning my sense of belonging within academia. Emotionally indescribable at times, it felt like a weight of inadequacy in a space that I feared and had sought refuge from. With tears flowing, I remember the day I called my sister-scholar to share with her that I felt that I just was not made to be in these academic spaces. She listened, she was present, and then she worked with me to determine the next steps for remaining in the program. Her words not only affirmed me but centered my *mattering* in the Ph.D. journey- a conversation that I will never forget.

After a series of phone calls- and planning sessions, I found a new advisor. As the site supervisor for my research assistantship, she had always been so supportive. She would become my chair and guide me through the remaining processes of my journey- which included shifting into a new academic program, establishing a new committee, and taking introductory doctoral courses that were required in my new academic home. In this transition, however, even amidst my new advisors unwavering support, my confidence had been shattered from the years of seeking validation from a chair that continued to suggest marriage and mothering just was not in the cards for an aspiring Black woman Ph.D.

The Finale: **Her Grace Is Sufficient in 2018**

I remember being so fearful in my second pregnancy because of the lingering realities that had framed my entry into mothering in academia. By the time I was expecting my daughter, I was one year in, having formally switched to my new chair and committee. Switching advisors was such a tumultuous experience that left me feeling completely defeated in my doctoral journey. Even with those around me who had become my lifelines of support in this pivot, I could not shake the words I had been told directly by my original advisor that my writing quality had "changed" since the birth of my son. I felt that I was not cut out for this kind of work.

Internally, I felt like my mothering identity was not being given the autonomy to equally sit alongside my emerging scholarly identity. The opposite of what we gain in centering a motherscholar framework, my mothering overshadowed the connection to my scholarly identity, which made me feel as if I had to work twice as hard to show that having kids had not had any effect on my work ethic and intellectual rigor. I was not publishing like those around me, or going to conferences for professional networking, because if I was not in class or at my research assistantship, I was tending to my home.

But even with all these ideas swirling around me, I remember the relationships and community that formed and filled me. My saving grace in this portion of my journey was community. Community and relationship with a new chair, whose gentle nudges and ethics of caring assured me that she had mentored several motherscholars over the years and was one herself. Community with my now fully established network of Blackgirl sister-scholars that had rallied around me, wiped my tears, let me sleep on their couches when the pregnancy tiredness kicked in, and were fully present for all of me and my family.

It was at five months pregnant with my daughter, in my sixth year of the journey, that I would defend my dissertation on the first floor of the College in front of my committee, my husband, and several classmates and peers.

A Blackgirl Motherscholar Homeplace

In embodying my own Blackgirl motherscholar identity, I leaned very heavily both inward through my *motherwork* (Collins, 1994) and outward in the spatial centering of what hooks (1990) defines as my *homeplace*. The homeplace provides a lens that offers language for facilitating meaning-making within contemporary Black family narratives. This is the language for how my family operationalized as a site of joy, resilience, and resistance during such a tumultuous experience. The role of my husband and my child[ren] walking with me in my journey created a sustained space, where my racial resilience and Black mothering was affirmed. hooks (1990) posited the homeplace as a space where values and beliefs are embedded in the stories that are told intergenerationally. These moments of storying lived experience in the home and other spaces of sanctuary- which were self-created (other)homeplaces outside of the home shaped what I now share as my Blackgirl joy and resilience during my process.

My experiences in these spaces informed my positionality of marriage and family as motivation to persist rather than hindering or limiting- as was suggested by my first chair. The homeplace created space for acknowledging that while balancing coursework, teaching, and parenting presented its own challenges, what I found most difficult was the isolation in embodying my motherwork, in addition to openly and authentically within critique (imposed and internalized). These tensions are what propelled me to press into the homeplace and (other) homeplaces, where I had to cultivate community so I could move from surviving in the Ph.D. process to thriving in it. It was in the same shifting towards thriving and not just surviving, that I went back to my beginning, who I was in name and identity.

What was important to me was being able to name this moment on my own, through my own experience. That is what was central in the communities I had built for sanctuary, and what I needed to foreground across various aspects of my lived experience. I had come to learn that the second important point about our identities can be self-chosen. It was ok to be the gifted Black girl in the classroom, even if I was just one of two; and it was also ok to desire and seek out culturally diverse spaces for the other parts of me that enjoyed a community that affirmed the whole me. Through reflection and introspection, we are able to make the choice to trouble the implications of socialization for how we decide to see ourselves. Other people may give us names (e.g. our parents) and labels (e.g. gifted, society) but an internal identity and self-concept should come from us. For me, an identity represents how we perceive ourselves and how we

TABLE 6.1 Conceptualizing My Blackgirl Motherscholar Homeplace

Conceptualizing My Blackgirl Motherscholar Homeplace

Homeplace (hooks, 1990) "A site of resistance and liberation" (p. 42). The homeplace and (*other*)homeplaces, [sites outside of the home that were home] umbrella my conceptualizations below towards tenets of Blackgirl Motherscholar Homeplace.

Motherwork (Collins, 1994)	Motherscholar Framework (Matias, 2011; Howard et al., 2020)	My Blackgirl Motherscholar Identity
Motherwork and Physical Survival Motherwork is essential to individual and community survival through centering the types of mothering relationships and engagements that assure well-being across generations.	**Motherscholaring as risky scholarly community and defiant learning** "We consider what it means to motherscholar. We talk, we read, we write, we collaborate, Because motherscholaring cannot be done alone. It is always a risk, because, Motherscholaring is defiant learning" (Howard et al., p. 8).	**Blackgirl Vulnerabilities and Affirming Spatiality as Physical Survival** Ex: Navigating the tensions in my doctoral journey (supports in mentoring, isolation, balance, etc.), I often needed spaces of love and positivity (personal and professional) in my vulnerability. These spaces offered affirmation, healing, and peace.
Motherwork and Power For women of color, choosing to become a mother challenges institutional policies that encourage the White-middle class and centers empowerment in strong, dynamic, indigenous culture as central to BIPOC women's social constructions of motherhood.	**Motherscholaring as epistemology** "As motherscholars who are educational researchers, To rethink what it means for our work to– be answerable to learning, knowledge, and living beings' needs? (Patel, 2016)" (Howard et al., p. 8).	**Blackgirl Relationships as Reclamation of Power and Ways of Knowing** Ex: As Blackgirls we have to create a community [on our campus and beyond] for ourselves dedicated to inclusion, appreciation, empowerment, and capacity. This was central to my Ph.D. journey and created spaces for my way of knowing to be received as a fund of knowledge in the Blackgirl Ph.D. process.

(*Continued*)

TABLE 6.1 (Continued)

Motherwork and Identity	Conceptualizing My Blackgirl Motherscholar Homeplace Motherscholaring as representation of scholarly thought and accountability	Blackgirl Resilience and an Embodied Motherwork in the Homeplace
The women of color's motherwork requires reconciling the preparation to cope with and survive within systems and consider the skill sets for challenging them at the same time.	"Instead, [as motherscholars] we are interrupting ourselves, learning alongside our children (Matias, 2016), Disrupting the status quo, We seek answers and answerability" (Howard et al., p. 9).	Ex: In pursuing my Ph.D. I was able to embody my *motherwork* as resistance to protect my family, myself, and to now expose the many tensions women in academia typically navigate in being discouraged from having children until you've achieved tenure.

want other people to perceive us, and a label is a descriptor given to us by others often based on their stereotypes. But, an embodied gifted Blackgirl motherscholar identity validates the voices of those othered in the mainstream Ph.D. process. In utilizing alternative ways to create independent self-definitions and self-valuations, I was able to rearticulate myself and my realities through my own narrative (Collins, 2000; Craddock, 2015).

Through this rearticulation and centering of authentically grounded self-definition, I capture that and articulate introspection assisted in the conceptualization of my Blackgirl motherscholar homeplace. Below I provide a visual, which organizes the relationships present across both frameworks of motherwork (Collins, 1994) and motherscholaring (Matias, 2011; Howard et al., 2020) and that informs and shapes what I articulate as my Blackgirl Motherscholar identity.

Blackgirl Vulnerabilities and Affirming Spatiality as Physical Survival

Collins (2000) states that increasingly present in the consciousness of being Black in White-dominated majority spaces, is the fundamental reality that one's experience is oftentimes invisible and undervalued. I learned early on that the doctoral journey required some level of vulnerability. At the end of the doctoral process, you carry the label of scholar and in the journey, you are working towards refining, strengthening, and becoming the expert within your respective discipline. This vulnerability, however, was negotiated differently for me through my racialized and gendered identity as a Blackgirl.

As a Blackgirl motherscholar pursuing my Ph.D., spaces for vulnerability were central, more specifically through an intersectional centering that acknowledged the systemic and structural silencing that persists in academia. This is further convoluted when I add in my mothering identity. This additional strand of lived experience, coupled with the tensions of racialized and gendered experiences in the academy, truly called for moments for affirming spatiality that could support and complement the experiences I would continue to navigate in my journey.

Motherwork is filled with joys and challenges. For moms working towards a graduate degree, pursuing their dreams can introduce a whole new set of challenges as well as unexpected joys. I am most proud that after having my son at the end of my second year of coursework, I still persevered. It was the spaces of vulnerability to just "be" myself that catalyzed those moments for me.

I often debated if I could do it all, and yet, here I am, still vulnerable and still proud that I can help further the conversation on campuses surrounding graduate students and junior faculty who are parents. As Blackgirls we must create a community [on our campus and beyond] for ourselves dedicated to inclusion, appreciation, empowerment, and capacity. Our racialized and gendered identities within the professoriate, in my experience, require that kind of community for survival. This was the necessary centering I needed in the high-achieving/gifted academic spaces I navigated before the Ph.D., and that I needed even more so during the doctoral journey.

Although having a child meant that I completed a couple of years later than anticipated, I reflect on my dissertation and journey as sacred and central, as my research agenda is also rooted in the experiences of Black mothers.

There were and still are many hard moments as a Blackgirl in academia, but I know I am called to this work, and I know deep down that, despite the challenges and obstacles, this is where I want to be. This is the life I want for myself. With this mindset, I was able to push through the difficulties because my work had purpose and meaning. My vulnerabilities and the Blackgirl spaces of affirmation created through community helped me make sense of this when I had challenges articulating for myself.

We find shelter in these spaces of vulnerability, and it is imperative for us to have our own sacred spaces- where we can unload the burdens of what the world expects us to be. Affirming spaces for families and sisterhood, to be understood for us, by us.

Blackgirl Relationships as Reclamation of Power and Ways of Knowing

I do believe my Blackgirl motherscholar identity is what has shifted my positioning from surviving to thriving in academia. With a dedicated support system including encouraging and understanding sister-scholars, faculty mentors, adequate healthcare and affordable childcare options, flexible scheduling, and systems in place to provide substitute instructors to cover classes for mothers recovering from childbirth, amongst other institutional adjustments, it can be done- and with joy.

My reflections, however, also note that universities can make it difficult for a lot of women, if these intersections of identity are not considered for their complexities. These are still spaces of tension in academia in my Blackgirl motherscholar identity, as I navigate promotion and the professoriate with two Black children, amidst the realities of the COVID-19 pandemic era and the racial tension and trauma that they are faced with daily. There needs to be a shift in the way universities and colleges view mothers. Instead of assuming that mothers are not fully committed to their scholarly "babies," if they have children. Graduate schools should reach out to women and work with them to create university systems that work for all students and faculty, regardless of their family status. Continued discussion also needs to be had to acknowledge that mothering experiences are negotiated differently at intersections of race and gender. Intersections of lived experiences that warrant and protect some experiences of mothering, but not others. In my case and in this journey, it made sense to put my homeplace, motherwork – and my sanity – first, and every motherscholar should be given the autonomy without tension to thrive in academia, home, and beyond.

Prioritizing Blackgirl relationships becomes a reclamation of power. A reclamation of power that centers Blackgirl motherscholars lived experiences as valid, essential, and needed.

Blackgirl Motherscholar Resilience and Embodied Motherwork in the Homeplace

My homeplace sustained me, my family, and my children. In pursuing my Ph.D. I was able to embody my motherwork as resistance to protect my family, myself, and to now expose the many tensions women in academia typically navigate in being discouraged from having children until they have achieved tenure. Those who go forward with parenthood anyway are often punished for their choice by a culture that looks down on mothers and expects their research to suffer (Mirick & Wladkowski, 2018).

This environment, without the sanctity of the homeplace, can offer expectations that often shape reality in challenging ways for Blackgirl motherscholars. Female graduate students and postdoctoral fellows who become mothers are more than twice as likely to leave academia, (Miller & Riley, 2021), and mothers with young children who stay in their fields are 132% more likely to wind up in low-paying adjunct positions compared to men with young children (Miller & Riley, 2021). A rigid academic timeframe and structure makes it difficult for mothers to achieve balance in their work and family lives, to lean into their motherwork and homeplaces of protection. This can also be worsened by the disdain and condescension that characterizes academia's views toward motherhood. These discourses are why Blackgirl motherscholar narratives must be centered and understood. I was privileged to have been able to lean into my homeplace and embodied motherwork as the response and disruption to these very ideals.

Conclusion

In closing, as I recognize that the journeys we travel are also often for those who chart their experiences after us, I am left with the wisdom of encouraging all Blackgirl motherscholars to stand confident in their spaces both within and beyond academia and within their *homeplaces*. Blackgirl motherwork continues to raise, transform, and impact generations. We see this in the many exemplars of Blackgirl motherscholars that continue to break barriers, boundaries, and change the world through their research, practice, and scholarship. This is a reason we collectively chart spaces and places that can uncover, uplift, and disrupt harmful discourses that impact the pathways and realities of Blackgirl motherscholars epistemologies. To recognize this collective effort in moments of unknown or angst offers strength for standing confidently in what you have concluded is the need for yourself, your family, and your professional aspirations. This type of intention and support is vital for inclusion and thriving for Blackgirl motherscholars. As a gifted Blackgirl motherscholar, these are the kinds of mechanisms of support that are needed and central to current and future aspirations in academia.

Know Blackgirl motherscholar, you are uniquely qualified to overcome difficult challenges and through our embodied *motherwork* and Blackgirl *motherscholar* identity we can continue to advance our collective storytelling methods and community-building needs as outlets for our truths.

We can also lean confidently in the spaces we create along the way for protection and resistance, our Blackgirl mothescholar *homeplaces*.

It is time our culture stopped blaming our mothers and started listening to Blackgirl mothers' voices.

References

Boylorn, R. (2013). *Sweetwater: Black women and narratives of resilience*. Peter Lang.
Boylorn, R. M. (2016). On being at home with myself: Blackgirl autoethnography as research praxis. *International Review of Qualitative Research, 9*(1), 44–58.
Butler, T. T. (2018). Black girl cartography: Black girlhood and place-making in education research. *Review of Research in Education, 42*(1), 28–45. https://doi.org/10.3102/0091732X18762114
Cahill, L. (2021). *The space love maps: A Blackgirl legend in three plots*. CUNY Academic Works.
Collins, P. (1994). Shifting the center: Race, class, and feminist theorizing about motherhood. In E. Nakano Glenn, G. Chang, & L. R. Forcey (Eds.), *Mothering: Ideology, experience, and agency* (pp. 45–65). Routledge.
Collins, P. (2000). *Black feminist thought knowledge consciousness and the politics of empowerment*. Routledge.
Craddock, K. (2015). *Black motherhoods: Contours, context and considerations*. Demeter Press.
Dillard, C. (2000). The substance of things hoped for, the evidence of things not seen: Examining an endarkened feminist epistemology in educational research and leadership, *International Journal of Qualitative Studies in Education, 13*(6), 661–681. https://doi.org/10.1080/09518390050211565
Dillard, C. (2022). *The spirit of our work: Black women teachers (re)member*. Beacon Press.
Durkin, K. (1995). *Developmental social psychology: From infancy to old age*. Blackwell Publishers.
Glenn, E., Chang, G., & Forcey, L. (1994). *Mothering: Ideology, experience and agency*. Routledge.
hooks, b. (1994). Confronting class in the classroom. *The critical pedagogy reader*, 142–150.
Hill, D. C. (2019). Blackgirl, one word: Necessary transgressions in the name of imagining Black girlhood. *Cultural Studies ↔ Critical Methodologies, 19*(4), 275–283. https://doi.org/10.1177/1532708616674994
hooks, b. (1990). *Yearning: Race, gender, and cultural politics*. South End Press.
Howard, J. Nash, K., & Thompson, C. (2020). Motherscholaring: A collective poetic autoethnographic inquiry. *International Journal of Qualitative Studies in Education*. https://doi.org/10.1080/09518398.2020.1852486
Lapayese, Y. V. (2012). Mother-scholar. In Y. V. Lapayese (Ed.), *Mother-scholar: Transgressions* (Vol. 85). SensePublishers. https://doi.org/10.1007/978-94-6091-891-9_1

Matias, C. (2011). Motherscholar panel. Annual Meeting of the American Educational Studies Association.

Miller, K. E., & Riley, J. (2021). Changed landscape, unchanged norms: Work-family conflict and the persistence of the academic mother ideal. *Innovative Higher Education*. https://doi.org/10.1007/s10755-021-09586-2

Mirick, R. G., & Wladkowski, S. P. (2018). Pregnancy, motherhood, and academic career goals: Doctoral students' perspectives. *Affilia*, *33*(2), 253–269. https://doi.org/10.1177/0886109917753835

Phoenix, A., & Woolett, A. (1991). Motherhood: Social construction, politics and psychology. In A. Phoenix, A. Woolett, & E. Lloyd (Eds.), *Motherhood-meanings, practices and ideologies* (pp. 13–28). Sage Publishers.

Patel, L. (2016). *Decolonizing educational research: From ownership to answerability*. Routledge

7

TRUTH BE TOLD

Testimonies of A Black STEM Health Scholar-Wife-Mother

Miranda Hill, Ph.D.

A Black Girl from Kansas: The Educational Origins of Coping with Racial Violence, Imposter Syndrome, and Giftedness

Brutal Beginnings

Truth be told, my orientation to education was racially violent. My family was on the tail-end of the Great Migration of African Americans from the U.S. South, to Midwestern and Northern areas for the promise of a less racist society. Upon settling, they found their illusions of equity and economic prosperity were crumbling like grains of dirt into an anti-Black dustbowl. There, I was born to my single mom in a small town in Kansas, where I eventually attended kindergarten and first grade in an adjacent rural town. This town, ironically called Haven, was then known for its hidden, yet thriving, Ku Klux Klan stronghold. I was the only Black child in my grade and one of six Black children in the entire school system (two of whom were my aunts).

I do not remember a lot of other life events that happened around the tender age of six, but I do remember the teachers and kids mocking me because I did not know my alphabet. I remember being asked if I tasted like chocolate and going to sleep at night wanting to wake up one day with flowing blond ringlets. I remember arguing with children who were determined to identify me as "Black" as I held up a crayon to show them that I was, indeed, Brown. I remember standing my ground when they repeatedly told me that I did not have a father because he did not live with me. I remember being openly called a "nigg**" daily on the playground,

DOI: 10.4324/9781003292180-8

without opposition from supervising teachers. I remember calling other white classmates "nigg**s" and not thinking anything of it because I did not know that it was a derogatory term reserved for the one person in our class with brown skin. I most clearly remember the day that my most hateful bully lied to our teacher and told her that I burned him with a glue gun. I remember her reacting by yanking me by the arm into the hallway with the bully. I remember her handing him the glue gun and prompting me to hold my hand out so that he could burn me with it. I cannot remember why I never told my mother what happened. I also cannot remember if the story was suppressed by my teacher telling me not to say anything about it, or my own fears of getting in trouble with the teacher. Either way, I am 99% certain that the truth of what I experienced would not have brought about justice for me. Nonetheless, I was soon out of there once my mother caught wind of a song that I learned from my classmates that sordidly remixed "jingle bells" to say, "granny got a trigger and shot a nigg**, and they began to cry." In the middle of the school year, we transitioned from the cozy bedroom that we shared in my grandparent's mobile home, to a little house just down the street from my new elementary school.

Truth be told, my palpably painful experiences with racism via the infliction of bodily harm, taunting, teasing, and racial epithets dissolved into a distant memory. Yet, the avoidant coping via physical and emotional relocation served as a lasting framework for how I would navigate racial violence in educational institutions throughout the rest of my life. Whenever assaulted, I learned how to peacefully move on, and focus on what I could control, knowing that justice was not promised to me in educational settings.

New Beginnings, Emerging Gifts, and Imposter Syndrome

At my new school, I had a teacher who poured her soul into helping me read at the age of seven. The year after I left her second grade class, I was offered to advance to a fourth grade reading level, with the possibility of moving further up. My fears of being taunted and teased by older kids drove my resistance to advance to the next level. Yet, once my mother knew that I was gifted, she accepted nothing less than excellence. Every A- and misspelled word was interrogated. While I excelled under her academic expectations, I hid my grade reports from my mother, solely due to the unsatisfactory behavioral comments from teachers. These comments read to the tune of, "Miranda does excellent work. However, she gets up and disturbs other children when she is done with her classwork." Irrespective of their intentions, my teachers chose to paint me as a disturbance, without recognizing that I was unchallenged by my learning environment.

Thus, I denied and rejected the notion that there was anything academically exceptional about me. I would ace all stages of competitive events, up to a final math or spelling competition, only to self-eliminate at the last minute. I did this multiple times, right up until the sixth grade. It was then that I vividly recall my second grade teacher (the one who taught me how to read in the second grade and had been secretly keeping track of my accomplishments throughout elementary school) coming out of nowhere and pulling me aside as I stepped out of line for the school-wide spelling bee. She looked me directly in the eyes and chastised me for quitting academic challenges before reaching the final stage. I did not understand it at the time, but it was good ole unadulterated tough love. She saw my potential and wanted me to win. However, what she did not understand (and neither did I at the time), was how horrifying failure was to me in the midst of being singled out.

Truth be told, the seeds of imposter syndrome, borne out of transitioning from educational delays due to racism to giftedness and a lack of visible academic success among Black people had already taken root of my views at an early age. Whether I won or failed, the pressure of standing out more than I already did, as one of no more than five Black children in my school, was too much to bear. My fear of inevitable failure and exclusion eroded my confidence. The imposter syndrome remained a thorn in every elevating step during my educational career, stimulating fear and panic due to the lack of representation of Black scientists and professors in my Ph.D. program, in addition to, further experiences of endemic intersectional racism and sexism in academia.

Captivated by Science: Intrinsic Drive as a Compass and Perseverance Tool in Predominantly White Institution (PWI) Educational Settings

I continued to excel with quiet confidence throughout middle and high school, despite the persistence of racism and educational setbacks. Out of all subjects, science came the easiest to me. In the seventh grade, I conceptualized and designed an experimental trial, during which I carefully monitored and controlled all aspects of growing pea plants, save for the growing medium (potting soil, clay, and sand). I carefully followed the scientific method, hypothesizing that a pea plant would grow to a greater height in potting soil. I dedicated effort to maintaining uniformity in the plant pots and the amount of growing medium. I carefully placed the pots on the same windowsill to ensure that they received an equivalent amount of sunlight. I used my grandmother's coffee cup to administer an exact amount of water to each red clay pot on a schedule. I remember the exhilaration of seeing the first pea sprouts pierce through the soil and into the daylight. With my index finger and the gentlest touch, I delicately unfoiled the tender sprouts to measure growth with my wooden ruler and recorded the day and time in my composition notebook. We did not have a computer at home, so I tagged along with my mom to the office where she worked on a Saturday and used her computer to play around with different chart features that could show off the differences between the plants. As the science fair approached, I selected a vibrant and warm color scheme with brick red, rust orange, mustard yellow, chocolate brown, and fern green for my large tri-fold poster board. I cut out plant pots, springy plant sprouts, and leaves from construction paper and pasted them along with my bar charts beneath a catchy title and pun ("Soil Matters") that played on the fact that soil was matter, and that the type of soil used to grow plants, did in fact, matter. On the day of the experiment, I set everything up to my meticulous liking—with the tri-fold behind the plants and my composition notebook. And in true fashion, *I left*.

I did not find out until Monday that I was one of two students who won a grand prize. I smiled as I cradled the shiny blue first place ribbon in my hand, knowing that I won without the intention of winning. The scientific process stirred up something inside of me. *I was captivated by it*.

Truth be told, tuning into my intrinsic drive, without being attached to external validation became my compass for gauging my success. My satisfaction with what I was doing, and how I was doing it later became an antidote for imposter syndrome. Checking in with my intuition and feelings, while doing my best allowed me to persevere through moments of questioning whether I was capable or qualified to be in a Ph.D. program. It allowed me to find an emotional middle-ground whenever my internal critic allied with the criticism of others in an attempt to derail my progress. Awards came and went, but the work that added meaning and satisfaction to my journey endured.

Locating My Place in STEM Health: Learning Survival Politics in Preparation for PWI Program Success

Finding Purpose and Passion In-between

Despite possessing a passion for women's health and personal traits that screamed "scientist," I lacked knowledge of the range of career options available to me in health sciences. I also did not have any role models or wherewithal to identify mentorship. In my community, if a child loved science and health and did well in school, they were encouraged to become a physician. No one knew what public health or population health sciences were. Thus, I settled my focus at a young age on becoming a women's health physician. Fulfilling my and my mother's dream, I attended Spelman College—a historically Black liberal arts college for women in Atlanta, GA. I majored in Biology with a pre-medicine track, participated in a summer internship at a medical school, joined the health education club at Spelman, and shadowed physicians from my parent's church. As the career path and overall life that I was pursuing became revealed to me through exposure, I began to develop a nagging feeling that medicine was not where I wanted to be. I did not want to treat health conditions or the symptoms of those conditions. My liberal arts HBCU curriculum stimulated a desire to mobilize systemic reform to prevent community health issues through education and social justice. With the waning motivation to attend medical school, I graduated just right before the 2008 economic recession with no clarity on my future direction. To put food on the table, I took a job as a server, in hopes that one day I would figure it out.

Truth be told, the survival politics that I learned from my early childhood environment were refined during my years of serving people in restaurant settings, to ultimately shape how I would deal with power structures in my Ph.D. program. The social conditioning derived from growing up in a predominantly white social environment in Kansas, while being nested in a predominantly Black social network, encouraged a practice of code-switching my language and personality to assimilate with others. I knew white culture from my teachers, friends, and macrosocial environment. I was also well-versed in the vernacular and mannerisms innate within Black culture, and witnessed how my family adapted their demeanor to interact with one another and non-Black people in culturally acceptable ways. Being a server allowed me to put into practice what I saw. I learned how to adapt myself and code-switch to please customers. I was bubbly to people who wanted me to be bubbly, and I was quiet and chill with people who only wanted me to do nothing more than my job. After initially erupting into tears over overblown reactions to things that I could not control (like the restaurant being out of goat cheese), I grew a thick skin and learned how to "regulate" my emotions. I learned how to respond to trivial requests with externally satisfactory responses and dismiss their condescending, racist, and sexist remarks in exchange for the maintenance of my income and tips. Later, I responded in a similar manner, as I encountered comparably unacceptable behaviors during my Ph.D. program.

As I waited tables, I maintained my passion for women's health and wanted to learn about other ways that I could help those who were most in need. One day, I built up the courage to call around to women's health organizations in Atlanta to see if they were looking for volunteers. I found a downtown clinic with a reproductive health mobile unit that needed a volunteer to help coordinate their preventive health screenings to engage with women who were experiencing housing instability, and I dove right in. I continued to search for opportunities to give me more exposure to careers in women's health that did not involve care provision and came across a young women's leadership training internship at another women's health center. It was here, as a founder of a women's health education training committee, that I harmonized my passions with my talents. It was there that I saw a Black Epidemiologist present on Black maternal health disparities during our seminar series. Completely inspired and enthralled by the ability to do this type of work, I pulled her aside for a chat about her career. That chat, which was initiated in the clinic, lasted for hours until we were standing in flickering parking lot lights. She explained her career path in great detail to me and answered every question that I had while affirming that I would be a great candidate for a Master's in Public Health graduate program. I walked away bursting with excitement about my future, and after my unplanned 5-year career hiatus, enrolled in the Master's in Public Health program at the Southeastern University's College of Public Health the following fall. I decided to immediately transition into the doctoral program in Health Promotion and Behavior after getting involved in women's health research and learning about how a Ph.D. would provide me with additional expertise to investigate and intervene in health disparities among women.

Can't Burn Me: New Beginnings and Application of Life Lessons Learned about Resilience, Coping, and Black Liberation in PWI Educational Settings

When I began my Ph.D. program, I had the home court advantage of already having faculty, staff, and students in my corner whom I had already met while in the master's program. They assured me of their unwavering support and sponsored me for recognition and opportunities. I was cheerful, agreeable, superficially unbothered, and genuinely grateful to have finally been plugged into a purpose that tapped into many of my strengths and desires. I was willing and ready to put the setbacks of the past behind me and step into my future as a social justice public servant and scientific pioneer in women's health promotion. My ability to conform and make people feel comfortable around me served me well for a little while. I was a hyper-visible and invisible token. Guided by subconscious wisdom, I sought to conduct myself in a way that minimized the potential for exclusion from various groups of people that I needed for achieving my goals.

Truth be told, my learning environment was a bewildering cocktail of toxicity intermingled with support. To make things worse, there was racial representation, blanketed with blatant oppression. My Ph.D. program cohort was predominantly Black. However, there were only two Black Professors in our Health Sciences program. I recall instances where someone of authority would cavalierly say something racially ignorant or jarring. We (the many Black Ph.D. students) would draw in a breath for composure, discreetly dart side glances at one another, as if to say *did they really just say that?* as the wave of shock and second-hand embarrassment passed over. I was accepted into prestigious honor societies that promised to offer opportunities through powerful social connections, only to be excluded from conversations through turned backs and darting eyes that would look around, above, and through me, directly into the familiar faces of good ole boys right behind me. Yet, my sister-scholar networks were an ever-present source of visible and tangible support that reassured me that I was not going through these things alone.

Aside from that, my five-and-a-half-year Ph.D. journey was pretty much the same as anyone else's. There were highs and lows. I easily excelled at many things and failed at many others. For every manuscript that I successfully submitted to a journal, there was another one that never saw the light of day. I switched major advisors in the middle and was prompted to change my dissertation topic multiple times, after spending countless hours developing concepts and proposals. Sometimes faculty would show up for me, other times they did not because they were overwhelmed by all the roles and responsibilities that they navigated. Once I realized this, I began to develop compassion for them. Outwardly, and somewhat inwardly, I prided myself on being an upbeat and confident social chameleon despite disappointments. One could say that all is well that ends well, but…

Truth be told, it was messy, and vulnerability was costly. These experiences of marginalization began to weigh heavily on me, and at times, imposter syndrome would erupt into a performance of over-confidence that I often saw emulated by the many people who constantly had to sell themselves in order to fund their positions through extramural grants. At times, I would go above and beyond to prove that I belonged because I did not feel safe within a competitive R1 environment that evaluated our progress annually according to outputs, versus the experiences that shaped our ability to be productive. The sum of it was harder than I ever expressed it to be because I did not envision a road map to "excellence" in the academy if I felt too deeply. As the cracks in the ivory tower were being exposed to me through self-enhancing arrogance, competition, betrayal, and discord, I slowly began constructing my own emotional wall against the glue-gunned academy (that operated much like the one that my teacher used to burn me in the first grade). It was in my participation in a five-year diversity fellowship that I was able to validate the toxicity I was experiencing by listening to similar stories from other faculty and doctoral students of color at PWIs across the nation. This lowered my expectations for equity. I no longer expected to receive any act of kindness from the people who outwardly pledged their lives to public servitude, diversity, equity, and inclusion. I saw through the optical illusions and pulled on the familiar cloak of numbness that I adopted in my days of waiting tables so that nothing that anyone could say or do could harm me. My mind's eye was steadied on the prize. I adopted the motivational tools of my ancestors who were more concerned about justice for others so that I could help through my work rather than focus solely on myself. Importantly, I credit my success in reaching critical deadlines to my vast and welcoming sister-scholar network that regularly scheduled late-night study sessions dedicated to holding each other accountable to "doing the work" while bobbing our heads in unison to neo-soul melodies, and Southern hip-hop rhythms. My sister-scholar network also enforced work-life balance through exercise challenges and impromptu happy hour sessions that were especially soul-replenishing on hard days. While this felt noble and kept me going, I did not realize how the emotional fortress that kept me safe, secure, and protected also restricted my ability to empathize with my Black Ph.D. sister-scholar network about what they were going through. Do not get me wrong, I would sympathize with the harsh and hurtful treatment expressed in vent sessions that began with "can you believe that…?" But I was limited in investing in the act of giving and receiving the softness that I could not give to myself. I felt the same as the other Black women who were striving to succeed when faced with unspeakable challenges. For many of us, our degree was a ticket to our wildest dreams for socioeconomic mobility and justice in health. We were entrapped in the psychology of survival through silence, because despite high representation, we were not promised liberation through any actions that we would consider taking.

First Comes Love, Then Comes Marriage, Then Comes the Baby, and Finally, a Ph.D.

Ph.D. STEM Health Student + Wife Intersectionality: The Benefits and Trade-offs of Love and Marriage

Love found me early on in my educational journey. Being able to confide in my husband about what I was going through was one of the many advantages afforded to me through a marriage. Our marriage was built on a long-term relationship that began when I was a Spelman student, and my then-future-husband was attending Morehouse. We met through mutual close friends who desperately wanted us to link up so that we could have double dates at the Café Intermezzo—a European-style coffeehouse on Peachtree Street in midtown Atlanta (this was the thing to do when we were in school). Despite my initial vow to rebel against, what I believed to be, uppity and bourgeois dating norms in the Spelhouse (Spelman–Morehouse) couple arena, our complementary personalities, love for family, and romantic connection eventually overpowered our friendship. We continued to date for many years after meeting, through career and life fluctuations. We got engaged after a three-year long-distance international relationship, just prior to starting our master's degree programs at Southeastern University. We married in the summer between my Master's in Public Health and my Ph.D. program. While our journey was not the substance of fairy tales, our strong friendship and commitment to one another became a foundation of courage to yield to a rollercoaster of life transitions, brought on through developing our career goals, marriage, going through graduate school together at our PWI, and having our baby.

As I was navigating the ups and downs of my Ph.D. journey, my husband listened and provided perspective and encouragement to rise above the things that tried to pull me down. As he finished his master's program early and began working a full-time job, I also had the privilege of having a source of income to offset the meager living stipends provided through graduate assistantships. This eased distracting concerns about whether I would be able to have enough money to pay rent or put food on the table throughout my program. Thus, the multiple forms of support that I received from my life partner allowed me to solely focus on furthering my career, compared to working multiple jobs or side hustles to generate income.

Truth be told, becoming a spouse while pursuing a time- and energy-consuming Ph.D. had its own set of challenges. The combined demands for learning while teaching, conducting research, and engaging in service, occasionally collided with the needs of my relationship. I immensely enjoyed having a life partner, going on date nights, and the comfort of constant companionship. However, there were times when I was so busy and overwhelmed with all of my Ph.D. program responsibilities that I could not be present. Likewise, there were many other times when prioritizing my partner and marriage was my saving grace. At times, our career paths also pulled in opposing directions. Just as I was searching to achieve my career goals, he was also working on his. We were exposed to tensions that our parents did not navigate, due to our dedication to carving out independent, ambitious, and purpose-driven career paths, while holding onto our love, hopes, and dreams into building a family. There were hard decisions and sacrifices on both ends because we knew that we were worth it. We adhered to our enduring motto to take things one day at a time—a motto that we adopted when we started dating. While challenging to learn how to balance the intersections of my identities and roles as a Ph.D. student and newlywed, in the end, I learned how to harmonize the two and find peace in the middle through independent and couples therapy, which in turn, strengthened our collective ability to establish our own norms, communicate, create, and adjust boundaries, and extend grace to one another.

Motherhood: The Reprioritization and Extension of Self, Strength, and Determination by Yielding to the Unknown

I have always wanted to be a mother before I wanted to be anything else. I took great care of my baby dolls and showered them with love and affection, as I wondered what it would be like to witness and experience the power of God creating life in my body. I knew some women stayed at home to take care of their babies and families. However, none of the women in my family had that luxury or desire. Somewhere along the way as I contended with thoughts about my career path, I began to develop an increasing fear that I might not be able to have a baby and do all the things that I wanted to do in my career. That fear grew with increasing intensity, as I had the fundamental pieces in place to enable me to become a mom while doing work that I was passionate about. When I saw moms in academia, I could not fathom how they met the demands of work and raising a child. Once I figured out that I was pregnant in candidacy, I dropped two elective courses just prior to my mid-term exams. I was nervous about how I would be perceived by the faculty in my upcoming evaluations. I also felt ashamed for quitting something without an explanation other than "because I wanted to."

Truth be told, I felt like I needed to take some time to prioritize my health. The part of me that knew about the high burden of maternal health inequities among Black women told the other part of me that wanted to soldier through my accelerated path to sit down and be quiet. Before my pregnancy, I was racing forward on all cylinders like the rabbit who was always running late in *Alice in Wonderland*. I was commuting one hour north of our home in Atlanta to teach and attend classes five days a week, attending clinical community advisory board meetings in Atlanta, presenting at as many national conferences as I wanted to, and applying to multiple predoctoral training fellowships that were all over the country. I harkened to the voice of my maternal instincts, and yielded to the uncertainty of how having a baby would impact my Ph.D. trajectory. I wanted to give my baby the best opportunity to thrive within a womb that was rested and fed, with the privileges that I had been afforded because of continuous funding and spousal support throughout my pregnancy.

Still, I did not disclose my pregnancy to anyone but my major advisor and a couple of my Ph.D. colleagues. My major advisor was completely unphased, supportive, and reassuring in all the ways that I wanted and needed him to be. I knew that he had a family, and was a self-proclaimed "lover of babies," and found him to be an overall empathetic and compassionate person. All of this—sadly mattered, due to the horror stories that I've heard about the lack of support and discouraging remarks made by other faculty advisors of pregnant advisees. My daughter was born in July, and I was back teaching in the classroom in August. There was no postpartum leave for graduate student mothers. So, in preparation for my child's birth, I transformed my two-day, in-person course into a hybrid in-person and online structure, so that I only needed to commute one day per week. My husband and I activated our village of local parents to help us take care of the baby when I had to teach or be away at school.

Truth be told, I did not have the language to put into terms what I experienced in adding "mother" to my identity, roles, and responsibilities, because I had so heavily anesthetized myself against the hope that I had control over how things would turn out on any given day. Motherhood was beautifully chaotic and having my daughter slowed me down in all the right ways. While I have heard of many mothers who just kept going, I became much more intentional and strategic about the things that I said "yes" to when I became a mom. I passed on opportunities that I would have never declined because they did not align with my priorities. My Ph.D. advisor and professional advocate bragged about how focused motherhood made me and encouraged me to bring the baby with me whenever I needed to have a meeting or conduct business on campus. *Motherhood was accompanied by a tough process of letting go.* I desperately needed to become more confident in my ability to be with the ebbs and flows of life. It taught me about the necessity of flexibility and adaptability in seasons of change and growth.

So, while I embraced growth, this brought on uncertainty. During the initial months of motherhood, I mostly worked alone whenever the house was dark and silent because my time to congregate and study with my peers was pressed upon by the demands of marriage and motherhood. When my baby's sleep patterns changed or when she popped up with a random rash or runny nose that required a doctor's appointment during my normal writing, research, or teaching time, I would feel temporarily frazzled about when or how I would get things done. However, watching her filled me with incomparable awe, joy, and pleasure in living. I eventually relaxed once I realized that each new challenge resulted in me becoming more resilient and capable of multitasking with efficiency. Things became much easier when I let go of my need to know how things would go and whether I would be able to do what needed to be done in order to succeed. While balancing motherhood, marriage, and school, I stopped worrying about my timeline or fears of not meeting milestones altogether, because I realized that my drive did not diminish, and my talents had already made room for me to do all the things that I wanted to do. With each passing day, I soaked it all in, gradually loosening the grip of fears and insecurities that prevented me from exploiting resources and reaching out to people for help. Overall, my thinking became much more flexible, and my focus shifted from doing a perfect job to doing the best that I could with what was on my plate for the day.

Conclusion

Truth be told, there were times when I was an outstanding Ph.D. candidate, and a not-so-great wife or mom. Yet, many other times, my focus was homed in on my family. Learning how to "mother" myself through movement, nutrition, sleep, meditation, and prayer was the most important empowering and humanizing part of my experience. There were times when my belief in God alone was my community. I clung to my convictions and allowed them to empower me when no one else was able to. As I became vast in whom I was becoming, I held on to the things that brought life and vitality back to me. I became less afraid of my future because I knew it was shaping me into all I was meant to be.

8
NAVIGATING THE DOCTORAL PROCESS WHILE EXPERIENCING TRAGEDY

Elizabeth Farrah Louis, Ph.D.

This chapter will depict the narrative of a daughter of immigrant parents who navigated challenges, academic systems, and distance from her native homeland of Haiti. Through my journey of pursuing a doctoral program in psychology, I encountered tragedies that influenced my educational path, personal and professional development, and service to my community. I am a Haitian-American, first-generation, cisgender woman who grew up in Miami, Florida, and had frequent visits to Haiti. My cultural heritage informed the intersections of my identities, while I also acculturated to American society. The lens that I look through has been colored by experiences of biculturalism and bilingual nuances.

My doctoral journey was uniquely orchestrated with intentionality to live in Athens, Georgia, Haiti, Boston, Massachusetts, and Rwanda. During this period, I faced hardships, learned lessons, earned awards, and relied on others for support and guidance. My faith and respect for traditional religion were my cornerstones in cultivating meaning and fulfillment. I will share Haitian proverbs that were instrumental for me in my doctoral process that may benefit other Black women.

Pa Janm Bliye ou Ayisyen (Don't Ever Forget You're Haitian): Early Life

My family originates from Leogane, Les Cayes, Port-Salut, and Saut-d'Eau, Haiti. My mother and step-father immigrated to the U.S. in the 1980s seeking economic opportunities. As the first born of five children, I can recall being immersed in Haitian culture. Haitian Creole was the first language that colored my world, because I learned Haitian proverbs and idioms, and communicated with members of my community – a trait that would benefit me tremendously in my understanding and engagement with my heritage especially in the field of mental health. I embraced markers that identified me as Haitian, by attending Haitian Creole/French-speaking churches, listening to *kompa* music, and remaining updated on Haitian news. In Miami, we even have a designated neighborhood called Little Haiti, which further provided affirmation and acceptance of my identity. At the same time, I recall subtle and overt messages from my parents to not "act like an African American" which translated for my young mind to wear my school uniform appropriately, refrain from cursing and listening to hip hop music, and not to get in trouble in school. Yet, African American students who saw me as part of the "boat people" who were risking their lives to cross the ocean to flee Haiti or perceived that I practiced Vodou to place spells on them. I sometimes felt out of place, even though I was surrounded by Black people; I could not quite figure out the underlying reasons as a child why children and adults felt so strongly about their beliefs. I was simply trying to limit any notice of me and follow the rules in order to keep people satisfied and attain relative peace.

Identity. One of my earliest memories that indicated that I was a Haitian girl was succumbing to the infamous three L's I weekly encountered– *Lakay* (home), *Legliz* (church), and *Lekol* (school). As a girl, I was deemed by my culture as someone who needed to be "protected," someone who was vulnerable and could get pregnant. My parents were very protective, to the point that they only allowed me to attend school or church-related activities. As the eldest, I took on adult responsibilities for our home. The roles that were left for me were to be a caretaker to my siblings, read my parents' bills, call to make appointments, be their translator, and make important medical and financial decisions for our family. These expectations stifled me, but at this point in my development, I had no agency. To cope, I would daydream of places that I would travel to in my head, watch world news to compare my life to others, read books, and sneak to play hide and seek with neighborhood children.

Church was considered not only a sacred place where families and friends came together to express our faith, but also a place where conforming, comparisons, and gender roles were reinforced. I observed that I needed to dress modestly and not speak up as a child. I was usually on my best behavior and polite. I appreciated the interactions I had with other youth during Sunday school, where we learned about the Bible or prepared for a youth show. One of my first understandings of relationships (e.g. respect adults and do not talk back; do not like boys, and you do not need friends) and gender differences (e.g. boys can be externally expressive, girls must be well-behaved; girls must be nice, speak softly, and cover their bodies) came from the church. I felt compelled to obey or else I would not be considered Christian enough.

When it came to my education, during middle and high school, I started to identify more with my Black racial identity, because as I excelled and received awards, my race was acknowledged more than my ethnicity. There were even times when school staff would misidentify me as African American or write my last name as Lewis. The ethnic stereotypes persisted in school amongst my peers, and I shrugged it off since I avoided confrontation at all costs. I was able to confront biases that my parents and others tried to instill in me by gaining diverse friends and learning from my peers. I realized I usually wanted to have my own personal experience, instead of taking someone's word for how they felt. I knew I had a mind and feelings and could make my own interpretations.

Although I was deemed capable to be in advanced courses, I was never considered for the gifted program, which consisted mostly of white students. Due to my parents not being actively involved in school and their perception that schools are responsible to make the best decisions for my education, there was not a big pushback from them regarding my eligibility. I once again had little voice to advocate for myself and did not know who to turn to when I became bored in class and finished my work quicker than my peers. Regardless of how many straight A's and awards I received, no one once approached me or my parents about transitioning to the gifted program. Unbeknownst to the Black Girl Magic in me, I continued to be high-achieving, and excel in computer programming in middle school and became a phlebotomist in high school. My tenacity, drive, boredom at school and home, curiosity for more, and seeing other Black children achieve bolstered my self-confidence.

Despite my internalized motivation, I recognized at an early age that I needed to be resourceful if I were to maintain a successful academic trajectory. Although I did not know anyone who attended college, I was curious enough to speak to guidance counselors. This led me to enter TRIO, a government-funded program for low-income students, with the University of Miami. I was very excited to be surrounded by high-achieving Black, Latinx, and other students of color with similar circumstances with an interest in going to college. I truly believed that it was this program that contributed to shifting my thoughts about my life of being more than the eldest Haitian girl in my family. I believed that a new chapter of self-exploration and access to resources positioned me to pursue the highest level of education. The journey to a Ph.D. was not easy, from initial disapproval from my parents that made me forfeit college scholarships, to turning my disappointment into motivation to transfer to Georgetown University.

Lòt bò dlo: Nuancing Distance

Lòt bò dlo is a term that is used in Haitian Creole for people of Haitian descent who are outside of their homeland. They are on the other side of the water that separates them from their family, friends, and country. Navigating and coping with a tough transition to an Ivy League school, being the only Black person in my class, and confronting Black students with higher socioeconomic status than me – brought about low morale. I second-guessed whether I belonged, and the Black professors who I turned to were attempting to overcome their own struggles at a predominantly white institution (PWI). I joined the gospel choir, which reinforced my spiritual beliefs and gave me strength. I also volunteered at school by teaching English to the same cafeteria workers who served me, to help me understand that there is more to life than taking classes. Also, I turned to serving my community, especially after the 2010 earthquake in Haiti, which killed hundreds of thousands of people. The distance between my immediate and extended family and friends became more apparent at the time of this tragedy, yet I went into crisis mode and responded to calls at the Haitian Embassy in Washington, D.C. and coordinated fundraisers. At the time, I did not realize that my interest in disaster mental health work was planted and would single-handedly connect me to an advisor who conducted research in weather psychology.

Prior to entering Southeastern University (Pseudonym), I applied to doctoral programs in psychology and did not get a single acceptance. This was devastating and I felt clueless of how to move forward. Without much thought, I applied to master's programs in mental health counseling because I observed white peers doing so. I was accepted into a program at Boston College and gained more knowledge and counseling skills. Being one of two Black students in the program, participating in research, and receiving mentorship from Black professors, I earned a master's degree and felt more confident to apply to doctoral programs.

With my interest in mental health and crisis response experience, I intentionally had a conversation with a faculty member who would select me to enter my doctoral program at Southeastern University. At the very beginning, my intuition nudged me to believe I will find time in my doctoral program to study in Haiti. Given that my advisor was a white man, I felt early on as a first-year doctoral student, the need to seek out mentorship from people who looked like me, hence why I found Dr. Guerda Nicolas, a Haitian scholar. After I contacted her, she saw my persistence and interviewed me to discern if I would be a good fit for her work in Haiti. It is crucial to not only have your primary advisor(s), because representation is important, also, seeking out other perspectives and sources of support throughout your doctoral process can be a lifesaver. There were times I did not feel understood and heard by my white male advisor, and we had different research styles. I knew that the comfort in not having to overexplain what the unique needs of Black and Haitian people and why cultural approaches were relevant to my clinical and research work was crucial for me mentally and emotionally.

With Dr. Nicolas, in the Summer of 2015, I traveled with her to Arcahaie to co-deliver a mental health workshop. That opportunity gave me a chance to learn more about mental health from this context, to use Haitian Creole to deliver that workshop, and this inspired me to do more community-based programs that used historical, cultural, and Haitian Creole vernacular. That field work created the foundation for the start of my international mental health work and demonstrated how the doctoral experience can be tailored to one's interest. At the same time, I continued to have open communication with my advisor and other professors in my program to not create any potential rift by having outside mentorship and experiences that were not traditionally included. I knew it was a risk but reassured my program of the relevancy of that experience. I ensured that I passed my courses and stayed on track to complete my Ph.D. on time.

Se Soulye ki Konn si Chosèt Gen Twou: Avek Kouraj, An Nou Fè Fas a Fas Avèk Trajedi (With Courage, We Can Face Tragedy Head On)

My second trip to Haiti led me to the southern region where in 2016, Hurricane Matthew, a category 5 storm with 168 mph winds, devastated cities and rural areas. You may be wondering, *Why do you keep going back to Haiti?* Let me give a brief history of my country, and my need to anchor my research, story, and work here. Haiti is known for its prolific historical events, courageous leaders, and compounded traumas. As the first Black sovereign country to gain independence in 1804 due to the consistent collectivism of Haitians and leaders such as Toussaint Louverture, Henri Christophe, Jean Jacques Dessalines, Marie Claire Heureuse Fèlicitè Bonheur, and Marie Jeanne Lemartinière, the nation of Ayiti (land of mountains) was birthed. Ayiti's perseverance influenced other uprisings across Latin America (Cuba, Venezuela), the USA, and other regions. Despite Ayiti's resilience, compounded traumas from earthquakes in 2010 and 2019, political instability, corrupted humanitarian aid, violence, poverty, and disparities across multiple systems have left the country in a state of heightened vulnerability.

During the post-disaster response to Hurricane Matthew, I connected with Dr. Florence Saint-Jean of Global Trauma Research, Inc. and the Haitian American Nurses Association. I participated in this humanitarian work to learn, serve, and put into practice the mental health skills that I had been learning from my doctoral program and other entities. It was an opportunity to adapt what I have learned in collaboration with Haitian agencies on the ground to respond to a tragedy. We visited different areas of the south, and set up health screenings at local churches/clinics during the week. Dr. Saint-Jean and I provided an adapted version of Psychological First Aid (PFA). PFA is a model to manage people's distress after a trauma and provide them with socio-emotional support. From this experience, it was very humbling to listen to heroic stories of survival, while also maintaining composure when sitting across from someone who lost their loved ones. One of the challenging parts of that work was the uncertainty of how and when people could move forward due to limited resources. I was tested as a clinician and doctoral student personally and professionally. I felt helpless and witnessed what post-disaster recovery looked like, especially in such a familiar place as home. This reminded me of my earlier experiences of crisis work and how timely response and context-specific resources are needed. I also became more critical of my educational preparation and reflected on additional training I needed in a more culturally responsive manner. I was eager to locate Haitian-led responses while recognizing the reality of their capacities and the need to reach out to the international community for aid. As a Haitian-American, I wondered if my few days of volunteer work were helpful or part of the common international response of swift and temporary support from outsiders, while those on the ground are left to come to terms with their realities and do what they can to survive.

Se soulye ki konn si chosèt gen twou (just because we hide our pain well does not mean we do not have pain), is a Haitian proverb that signified the temperament of my family affected by Hurricane Matthew. After my volunteer commitment, I visited my family and witnessed the structural destruction of roads, homes, and farms. It was difficult to see, and while they all were alive; the hurricane left its imprint on them and others in their communities. I vowed to help them rebuild their homes and promised to send supplies or money. From my $20,000 assistantship as a doctoral student, I knew I needed some support. I created a fundraiser and raised a little over $5,000 and received donations of supplies. I was so grateful for the generosity of the people in the area of Southeastern University, and friends from afar. I sent money to build one house and then I traveled to deliver the supplies in 2017. That experience taught me that even within a doctoral program, your role is not solely to be a student. There were roles and identities you had when you entered which may shift or change but nonetheless, being in a supportive doctoral program and community makes enduring hard times a little bit more bearable. I also learned that I could be stretched emotionally to be vulnerable, to let others in, and use a tragedy to inspire me to keep pushing through. After all, this degree was not only for me but for my family, friends, and those whom I served.

Sonje lapli ki te leve mayi w! (Remember the Rain That Sprouts Your Corn)

Do you remember the intuition I had at the beginning of my doctoral journey when I said I would study in Haiti? Guess what? I surely did! Ya girl was chosen to complete a U.S. State Department Boren Fellowship where I wrote a proposal on how Haitian mental health is important to U.S. national security. That fellowship bloomed the seed I planted prior to entering my doctoral program. During my 10 months of living, studying, and practicing field work in Haiti, I worked with Partners in Health, an international non-governmental organization. I immersed myself in the culture, developed professional relationships with colleagues, and worked with the hospital's mental health team. I took a class to strengthen my Haitian Creole language skills, learned more healthcare and mental health terminology, participated in planning workshops on trauma, and conducted research on self-care and religious leaders' perspectives of mental health that can inform hospital staff's engagement with them and patients. As a doctoral student, I lived my life on my terms. I was done with coursework and began to think about my dissertation. Living in Haiti made me reflect on life more deeply. I became more aware of the beauty and culture of the country, the daily challenges, and had endless rich conversations with family members, friends, colleagues, patients, and community members. I grew to have an appreciation for the slower pace, the reduced stress that I often felt when living in America, and became accustomed to not always having reliable cell phone service or the internet. I became more in tune with nature and quietness. I could not have developed a better plan than being in Haiti at the time, I truly needed it for my soul and spirit. I did remain in touch with my advisor and the grant program periodically, but I was mostly on my own and crafted my own schedule with leisure activities.

With the culmination of my education, knowledge, lived experiences, opportunities to serve in Haiti, and recognizing the gaps that exist in the literature, I decided to focus my dissertation on mental health providers who engaged in disaster work. Disaster work is an area saturated by organizations and international entities, mostly white workers. I examined race, gender, education, disaster experiences, and the perceptions people have of those they served. Some of my results demonstrated some of the differences that existed among people of color and whites, and I shared recommendations to inform the fields of psychology, disaster work, and humanitarian aid. I defended my dissertation on Haitian Flag Day on May 18, 2018. This proud moment was a great achievement for this once shy and quiet Black Haitian-American girl who was obedient and had limited agency. To have reached the dissertation stage, I relied on my Black peers for their support, such as reading my dissertation when my advisor was reluctant to. I received support from mentors outside of the program, my family and friends prayed and encouraged me. I personally engaged in self-care (e.g. read books for pleasure, traveled to new countries, exercised, prayed), dedicated myself to a research and writing schedule, reflected on my past disaster work experiences in Haiti, and envisioned the type of scholar I wanted to become once I completed my Ph.D.

During the last year of my doctoral program, the common question of "what's next?" came back after yet another educational commitment. I was not sure what I wanted to do, whether to go straight into clinical work or research, but once again this intuitive spirit in me confirmed once again that I would be traveling, and this time to Rwanda. After my graduation, I was accepted to the National Institutes of Health Fogarty Fellowship with Harvard University and Boston University Consortium. I conducted mental health research in Rwanda, traveled throughout working at different mental health sites, provided consultation on cases, and mentored colleagues and students. I even co-developed the national mental health guidelines for the COVID-19 pandemic. I appreciated all that I learned about the country, not only about its history of genocide but its culture, its people, their triumphs, and challenges. With this last fellowship to wrap up my doctoral journey, there are no words to express how grateful I am. My determination led me to look for resources for a Black woman such as myself, to strengthen my clinical and research skills, while also simultaneously pursuing topics that interested me. I am so appreciative of the friends who became my cheerleaders, advisors, grant reviewers, and self-care patrol officers who took care to ensure that I am taking care of myself and took my ideas seriously. With God, I dared to dream beyond what I could see and was flabbergasted every time.

Fanm Djanm: Knowing the Strong Woman

If there is a term that I could use to describe one of my characteristics, it would be *fanm djanm* which means "strong woman" in Haitian Creole. I embody this strength that pushed me when I faced uncertainty, when

I adjusted from being in a city to a small town, and when I was away from family and familiar support systems. I overcame imposter syndrome at Southeastern University and reminded myself I belonged. I was tested by comprehensive exams and an internship in yet another city. I had to maneuver program bureaucracy by identifying my allies, code-switching, understanding written and unwritten rules, and leveraging any privilege that I and trusted others had. Navigating through another predominantly white institution reminded me of the strategies that were effective for me such as finding my safe spaces, identifying Black student organizations, and learning about resources specifically for students of color. I could not have done any of this on my own without my in-person and virtual village.

I was usually balancing between surviving and thriving in my doctoral program. My support system of family, friends, mentors, colleagues and peers from different programs, and my church family were pivotal for my success and provided spaces for me to recharge. It was important for me to not only do research and take classes, but also to explore the areas around me. I found a local Haitian community, which affirmed my heritage and satisfied my cravings for Haitian food. I volunteered at a refugee organization, teaching English which addressed my need to serve regardless of the community I am in. For my own personal interest and desire to share one aspect of my culture, I created a Haitian Creole meetup group to learn that language. I made sure to stay plugged in with fellow Black sisters pursuing their Ph.D.s across different programs and appreciated these welcoming spaces for us to find community and support one another. This group was very special to me because we had many overlapping interests, similar backgrounds, and we saw each other for who we were. We were able to speak about our lives and some of the common areas that were relevant for us such as managing healthy relationships, attending to roles outside of being a doctoral student, responsibilities to our families, ways to maintain our sanity and wellness, and encouraging one another through countless foolishness, microaggressions, disrespect, and disregard for our identity. Through our sisterhood, we also showed out in support, promoted each other's work, and dedicated time to strengthen our bonds.

Without my faith, I am not sure how far I would have made it as well. My faith in God and in myself grew on different levels, such that it was a personal, yet spiritual journey. I found a routine that helped set my mindset and I used verses and created affirmations to uplift me regardless of whether I was having a good or bad day. I knew that my purpose for pursuing a Ph.D. was greater than me, this was for my family, my culture, the communities I served, and the possibility of so much more post my doctoral degree.

Lakou: The Desire for Sacred Community

We all have our *lakou*'s (sacred communal or familial yard). During my doctoral program, I was very intentional and mindful of who and what was in mine, in order to persevere and finish. I encourage every Black woman who is pursuing a doctoral program to reflect on what you need in your *lakou*, who can be a part of it, and what will keep it sacred for your doctoral season. I wish to leave you with a few Haitian proverbs that encouraged me or provided me with a check-in with myself:

- Piti, piti, wazo fè nich li. (Little by little the bird builds its nest.)
  - Every effort counts, you are building your branches to reach/exceed your goals; do not be dissuaded or discouraged by temporary setbacks.
- Bèl dan pa di zanmi. (Just because someone is smiling at you doesn't mean they're your friend.)
  - There may be one person or a few people who may have bias, may be disrespectful, or may not want you to excel, do not let their actions or inactions distract you from your mission and vision for yourself.
- Kay koule twompe soley men li pa twompe lapil. (A leaky house can fool the sun, but it can't fool the rain.)
  - You can fool others, but you cannot fool yourself or your *lakou* crew – be true to yourself and vulnerable with safe and affirming people.
- Woch nan dlio pa konnen doule woch nan soley. (The rock in the water does not know the pain of the rock in the sun.)
  - Do not compare yourself to others, we each have our paths to walk. Yes, you may have a starting point or intersect with others along your doctoral journey, yet your journey is uniquely crafted for you. Whether you must walk, run, or take a water break, keep moving.
- Pawòl gen zèl. (Words have wings.)
  - Develop affirmations, selected words, verses, quotes, or proverbs that speak to you – words can have such a powerful impact on your self-esteem, confidence, and what you are speaking into existence. Be mindful of the wings you are envisioning to fly.
- Si se Bondye ki voye, li peye fre ou. (If it is God who sends you, He'll pay your expenses.)
  - As a person of faith, this resonates with me. I trusted God to provide, and God did and added some extra sugar and spice to my milestones. Whether you adhere to a religion, spirituality, mindfulness practice, or humanistic beliefs – what is meant for you will happen. Do not get stuck in worrying about how it will happen – do your

part and release worry and go with the flow of your intuition/energy/vibe/manifestation.
- **Deye mòn gen mòn. (Behind mountains there are mountains.)**
  - The doctoral journey can be a beast. There will be challenge after challenge with valleys and mountain tops that you must climb. Do not let that shock your system to the point you become stagnant or afraid to fail. Part of this journey will include mistakes, lessons learned, and silver linings – hold onto those nuggets of wisdom and light.
- **Souke tèt pa kase kou. ([You can] shake your head, [but] do not break your neck.)**
  - I added this for kicks and giggles. Now we know that you will encounter people who are petty or have lost their damn minds, but do not overreact. Usually, my eyes demonstrate my stifled shock and I wait until I can debrief with a trusted person to fully express my discontent, laugh at the foolery I just witnessed or experienced, or receive some validation that I am not trippin'.
- **Tan ale, li pa tounen. (Time goes, [but] does not come back.)**
  - Yes, indeed the Ph.D. expedition can be tough sprinkled with some successes. However, do not forget to live your life, to indulge in self-care, interests, and hobbies. To take breaks, learn something new, or volunteer. Do not take these years for granted. Foster friendships and relationships that will exist beyond your doctoral years. This is supposedly the last opportunity to have a school lifestyle – take advantage of fellowships, scholarships, or trips that your graduate school or the international office has to offer. Explore the town or city around you and reflect on how you want to use this time besides pursuing another degree.
- **Men anpil, chay pa lou. (Many hands make the load lighter).**
  - Please remember that you are not alone. When life allows others to intersect with you for support and to be united with common interests and vision, this can be a very meaningful bond. The hands that can help you may be within and/or outside of your program (e.g., conferences, sororities, local organizations, faith-based entities, meetup groups, Black women-led functions, etc.). You do not have to carry everything on your own, let others in so that you can rest and be refreshed.

I hope you can use these proverbs or create your own that can be present in your *lakou*.

9

IMAGINING A NEW THING THROUGH ACTIVE DISRUPTION

Tools to Center Black Aliveness and Wholeness for Black Women in Doctoral Programs

*Shaquinta L. Richardson, Ph.D. and
Brittany N. Anderson, Ph.D.*

Brittany's Reflections: Untangling Myself from the Master Narrative

As Shaquinta and I had incubation sessions surrounding this work, we unpacked the layers associated with our lived experiences, the factions of the academy, and what it means to thrive. To do this, we had to contend with what it is, what it ain't, and the in-between. For me, that means how do I actively disrupt what the "gifted" label has been for Black girls and women, and what it means to fully reclaim and disrupt what it is presently. In critical spaces, I often find my work as an outlier because of the historical legacy of what gifted education has been for Black and Brown people. I understand the myriad of ways that critical scholarship/scholars contend with the problematic nature of gifted education, but we cannot throw the proverbial baby out with the bathwater. Meaning, our girls are in those spaces, classes, and programs, and need support to understand their identity, trajectory, and belonging in said spaces. I have had to feel my way in the dark many times, trying to understand the scope of my giftedness, but not having as many opportunities as my peers. I have had to learn and unlearn how perfectionism was so entrenched in my everyday experiences, which resulted in maladaptive coping strategies. These were societal factors of systemic and structural racism, but also learned behavior that started in the home and school program.

    The problematic nature of the field is something I continue to contend with, but I realize I must also move forward with the research agenda to understand the ways in which the gifted-identity label and trajectory has affected Black girlhood and womanhood. The scope of the academy was meant to be limiting, but what does it mean for me to embody liberation in my scholarship, teaching, and service, centering the needs of Black girls and women? One of the things that became so clear to me during our doctoral journey was the similarity of many of our experiences, and how giftedness was often our connector outside of race and gender. What does it mean for our girls currently? What steps are necessary for us to foster talent identification and development? What practices center homeplace, liberation, and praxis? Where is our homeplace in the academy and doctoral programs? I posit that our homeplace is amongst ourselves, *for us, by us*. However, for some of our sisters operating in siloed spaces, how does she arrive at this understanding for herself, while feeling alive? As Black women continue to do the work of liberation for ourselves and our sistren, we need tools and strategies to get us through in the meantime, while also focusing on futuristic practices. This chapter will provide such tools and strategies to aid in the protection and restoration of our womanhood.

Shaquinta's Reflections: Developing Our Tools to Dismantle the Master's House

As a practitioner-scholar, my focus on my personhood, above the degree, started during the doctoral process. I'm a therapist, coach, and healer. I made a decision during my first semester that regardless of how the process went, I wanted to come out on the other side of the journey as a whole person. Decisions I made from that day forward honored that decision and often left me feeling like I was not keeping up with my peers, including the other Black women I was in community with. My practice was an intentional rebellion, even if my mind and emotions sometimes felt less committed, less accomplished, and less successful. But what that decision and commitment to myself led to was the ultimate accomplishment, which was graduating feeling whole. Feeling like I got to fully experience my life in the midst of the process. Because of that rebellion, I now get to show and share with others what it looks like to honor our personhood and disrupt the beliefs and practices that dishonor and harm our personhood, our Black girlhood, in the name of progression.

As each of us shared our stories throughout this book, our intentions were to demonstrate the many ways our giftedness, gender, race, Socioeconomic Status (SES), and personal circumstances all coalesced to create unique, yet similar Blackgirl experiences. While being seen and feeling felt can be powerful, it often leaves us with the question of, "What do I do with this?" or, "How do I apply this to my life?" The wisdom situated in this chapter comes to you five-plus years post-graduation, and time has allowed us to expand our thinking across our career journeys. This chapter will answer those questions and provide tools, strategies, and resources to help you along your doctoral journey and beyond.

Self-Care

In recent years, the concept of self-care has become one of the most popular topics amongst Black women, particularly as we experienced the shut down and subsequent shift in labor practices following the COVID-19 pandemic. Self-care is defined as the process of establishing behaviors to ensure the holistic well-being of oneself. While the concept has become fairly popular in the social sphere, Black women in particular continue to struggle with the application on a regular basis and have not yet fully embraced self-care as a right for all of us. Historically, our value and humanity have been directly linked to our production, from slavery to the current times. Messages passed down intergenerationally prioritized safety and security, which meant working beyond our capacity to maintain employment, and ignoring basic emotions and physical needs to remain "low-maintenance" and easy to manage.

These messages and behaviors spilled over into the home-life as parents started this teaching early to keep their children safe, and to prepare them to have job security as adults. For the gifted Black girls and golden children among us, we also learned how to lighten the burdens of our own existence by not asking for too much, always doing well in school, and not getting into any trouble, which in Black households could mean anything from asking basic questions to advocating for ourselves when we were uncomfortable.

As a doctoral student, there are many pulls on your time, energy, and resources. Many of us enter the doctoral process with hopes of building our careers beyond what our parents had access to pursue. With those aspirations come pressure(s), but also hope for the future. Our determination and desire for the possibility of what a doctorate can mean is a strong motivator and can create a type of tunnel vision that leads us to ignore our basic human needs. Countless doctoral students express elevated levels of stress, sleep deprivation, malnutrition, isolation, and financial distress (Richardson & Lewis, 2020). In our minds, we justify these states as temporary sacrifices towards a larger goal. Although, all of us featured in this book know that the temporary part is a myth.

What we would like to offer here is that those self-sacrifices are not only unnecessary, but also counterproductive. What we have found through our own experiences is that the way to get through the doctoral process and actually come out the other side as a whole person, without high levels of post-doctoral trauma, is to develop practices and routines that honor your basic needs. As previously stated, the concept of self-care is a buzz socioculturally, but as we are describing it here, it is simply caring for yourself and honoring your needs. Ways to do this include:

1. Getting sleep regularly. Depriving yourself of sleep negatively affects your brain's function. It reduces your brain's ability to retain information and problem solve. Those few extra hours of reading and writing should be exceptions, not the standard. It is not noble nor commendable to deprive yourself of rest in the name of deadlines. Your work product will improve when you are well rested.
2. Drink water and move your body every day, throughout the day. Your body cannot survive on coffee. Sitting at computers is not good for your heart, lungs, bones, joints, muscles, or brain. At least 10 minutes a day of intentional movement can make a major impact.
3. No one ever graduated sooner by skipping meals. Develop an eating schedule so you do not go full days before having a meal. It is very easy to get caught up in the work. Set virtual and physical reminders if needed. Outsource if possible.
4. Incorporate leisure activities into your schedule. It is ok to have fun as a doctoral student. You are allowed to have a life outside of school. Anyone who tells you otherwise is perpetuating the same outdated academic hazing mentalities that caused so many to flee academia.
5. Hang out with people. Do work together sometimes. Don't do work other times. Isolation will negatively affect your mood and your overall mental health, which will then negatively affect your work. Nurture the relationships you had prior to the process that you would like to maintain. People's lives do not stop because you are getting a doctorate. If you want to be part of the journey, you have to make the effort to be involved.

Self-care does not have to take a lot of time, nor does it have to cost money, but it does have to be intentional and we do have to prioritize it as much or more than the degree. The practice of self-care expands beyond these basic steps and is unique for every person, but these foundational practices are a wonderful starting point. Another important aspect of caring for ourselves is protecting ourselves, and we do that by establishing boundaries.

Boundaries

In conjunction with developing practices to take care of your mind and body, it is also important to establish boundaries for yourself with the people you are connected with in school and your personal life. Boundaries are ways for you to signal to others how to access your gifts, your time, and your energy. No one is an unlimited source of any of these. We all have limits and it's up to us to inform people of those limits. Black women struggle with saying no in these environments out of fear. Fear of lost relationships, fear of lost opportunities, fear of retaliation, etc. It is that fear that leads to feeling burnt out and resentful.

While we can all recognize that we have to navigate these educational spaces with people who will blatantly disrespect our boundaries, it is often the fear of setting boundaries that causes more issues than the boundaries themselves. Confidently communicating your limits with tact and grace from the outset can prevent the shock of having to communicate them after people have gotten accustomed to a pattern with you. However, if you find yourself needing to establish new boundaries, confidence and grace go a long way.

Boundaries with family and friends are also important, as they may not always understand the weight of the responsibilities doctoral students carry, and may make requests of time and resources that may be difficult for a doctoral student. Learning to say no to people we love is one of the most difficult things to learn to do, but it is necessary. It is important to acknowledge your limits, communicate them, and trust that you are not the only source of support for the people in your life. Oftentimes, we become the resource because we are always available, which does not require people to seek other solutions. If you are, it may be time to help them find other sources of support in addition to you.

Dr. Nedra Tawwab (2021) created an amazing resource for setting boundaries called *Set Boundaries, Find Peace* which we would suggest you read to learn more about boundary-setting in multiple aspects of life.

Self-Trust/Disrupting Fear

Somewhere along our journeys we learn that we cannot trust our own thoughts, beliefs, and sometimes our own experiences. Because so much of our backgrounds have been based on survival, we are conditioned to constantly look for the threat and tend towards the perceived safest option. We learn not to ask questions when we need clarification, or pretend we know when we truly do not. We learn to keep quiet when we are being disrespected and mistreated. We learn not to ask for too much and accept whatever is given, even when it is nowhere near enough. Religious upbringing can also contribute to this, as faith traditions may teach us to not lean on our own understanding, and to constantly humble ourselves.

Coupled with gendered racism in academia and sociocultural conditioning, the result is often that Black women become afraid to acknowledge our brilliance and capabilities, as well as advocate for our needs.

As we identified with our stories, few of us came from heavily resourced backgrounds. Most of us "got it out the mud" if you will. This shared background allows us to understand how heavy the weight of getting out and never going back can be. We are driven by our survival. Our fear of failure. Our fear of being back in the same place we started. But if we constantly give in to that fear, we will never be able to get past the point of the hold that fear has on you. The more you make decisions based on those fears, the more tightly you stay bound and tethered to the source of them.

Every single Black woman who has made it to the doctoral level has a level of resilience you may not even be aware of. If you think back over your life, you have likely made it through many difficult situations. What often happens, though, is we focus on the struggle and decisions we made during those times, then judge those decisions based on the knowledge we have today. Oftentimes, when we look back at those situations and evaluate what could have been done differently with the level of knowledge and resources you had at the time, you realize you did the best you could. Once you can recognize that, you can see how well you have truly managed to navigate difficult situations. You can then allow yourself to shift the perspective to your strengths and ability to make good decisions with limited resources, because once again, you have made it this far. When you focus on what you have done, you identify a different pattern. One of capability. One of resilience. A pattern that points to the likelihood that no matter what the situation, you can trust yourself to figure out the next step, and the next, and the next.

Take a few minutes to sit down and think about everything you have ever accomplished or done well. Don't limit it to your academic or professional life, also include personal effects. Seriously, every single thing you can remember, no matter how small. Then write down every challenge you have faced and how you overcame it. Because we are so focused on getting to the next thing, we don't take inventory of what we have done, which makes it that much easier to doubt our abilities. Once you do this exercise, thank yourself for getting this far. Focus your thoughts on the characteristics and skills that helped you do the things on these lists. Compile the list of characteristics and then turn it into a list of affirmations about who you are and what you are truly capable of. Then remember, all this ish is made up. All these expectations and rules are tools of white supremacy. Then go on 'bout your business :-)

Perfectionism

Perfectionism is a maladaptive coping mechanism for managing our anxiety and fear of failure. Logically, we all know perfection is not real, yet we still strive for it anyway. Perfectionism shows up as feeling like you can't make a mistake or everything will fall apart. It's believing you have to show up a certain way physically and energetically at all times. It's feeling like you have to show up for everyone in your life whenever they call, regardless of what is going on in your life. It's trying to keep a spotless home even though you're physically and mentally exhausted. It's running that report one more time just to be sure after you've already done it 10 times. It's changing that sentence 17 different times before you submit because it doesn't feel right. It's searching for more and more information before making a decision. Perfectionism is driven by the fear of doing the wrong thing or making the wrong decision. Fear of failing, fear of losing your livelihood, fear of losing relationships. It's placing the weight of your life on every minute detail and decision.

In order to manage your perfectionism, you have to identify what drives it.

1. What is your goal?
2. What is the purpose of the task or activity you are working towards?
3. What is the objective requirement of that task or activity?

Then you must identify the fear.

1. What is the underlying fear?
2. What is the outcome you are trying to avoid?
3. What would happen if you made a mistake?
4. What would be the next step you could take?

Also, identify your role in the situation. Are you supposed to be an expert, or are you learning? If you are the expert, are you expected to know every single thing in relation to the topic? Spoiler alert: NO. For activities you tend to spin your wheels on, give yourself time, or establish limits and stick to them. For example, say to yourself, "I can review this 3 times before I must submit it." The main way to show yourself that perfection is not a requirement for your success is to do the scary things and show yourself it is ok. To be imperfect and wait for the response. Whatever it is, see the previous section about being able to figure it out.

Build Authentic Community

Lastly, learning to build community with other Black women was clearly one of the biggest and most impactful strategies for those of us in this book. We understand that it can be challenging to initiate connections. Even more so for the socially awkward amongst us. Still it is an important task and a worthwhile challenge to overcome. There are some spaces that promote competition and create an environment designed to make building community difficult, but we encourage you not to give into that and instead, focus on collaboration and support. This can even be done in private. Release any preconceived ideas you may have about relationships with other women, and allow yourself to be open to connecting with someone whose shared experience could be your balm of Gilead. That is not to say you have to force relationships with women you do not vibe with, but rather not shying away from getting to know someone new. Set up regular writing days. Talk through your research to get a perspective your professors cannot offer. Plan activities that do not involve school work. Encourage each other to take care of yourselves. Be a friend.

We recognize that not all schools have the same number of Black women doctoral students nor the connecting mechanism we had with the student organization. If that is the case, we recommend seeking virtual resources or programs in conjunction with national organizations within your field.

Additional Offerings

Below, we have included some journal prompts for reflection and affirmations to encourage you as you continue on this journey.

Journal Prompts/Questions for Consideration:

1. What are your beliefs about care for Black women? How do these apply to yourself?
2. What does it mean to YOU to be a gifted Black woman?
3. How did you see the women in your family caring for themselves? What would you have liked to see them be able to do?
4. When you think of the ways you show care for yourself, your needs, and your overall well-being, how do you feel about how you treat yourself?
5. What do you think will happen if you establish a boundary with someone you love?
6. What do you think will happen if you establish a boundary in your doctoral program?
7. How do your previous experiences as a gifted Black girl currently affect how you are navigating your doctoral program?

Reminders for our sisters:

1. We will never be enough for white folks who are determined to dehumanize and minimize us. The system is the problem. Not us.
2. I was always enough. Working myself into the ground to prove my worth to anyone is a capitalistic, racist, sexist notion and I am not willing to continue contributing to it without prioritizing my needs.
3. No one makes it in this world alone or without support. I can ask for help.
4. Sacrificing myself does not prevent failure. It ensures it.
5. The whole system is a mind trap that we must break free of if freedom is something we seek.

References

Richardson, S., & Lewis, C. (2020). *Conquering academia: Transparent experiences of diverse female doctoral students* (S. Richardson & C. Lewis, Eds.). Information Age Publishing Inc.

Tawwab, N. G. (2021). *Set boundaries, find peace: A guide to reclaiming yourself.* Penguin.

AFTERWORD

Black Gifted Women Journeying—*Together*

Chonika Coleman-King, Ph.D.

Drs. Brittany Anderson and Shaquinta Richardson have done something quite profound. They have brought together the voices of Black women to share the ways in which they navigated their identities as gifted/high-achieving, and how they made it through the arduous doctoral journey at a predominantly white institution—*together*. It is not a secret that institutions of higher education were not built with Black women in mind. In fact, many institutions in the southeastern United States are celebrating a mere 50 to 60 years since they matriculated their first Black student. I still find it hard to celebrate the tragedy of omission and exclusion, and despite doors subsequently having been opened, Black women continue to struggle to find their place in an academy that endeavors to preserve its racist, anti-Black, and male-dominated origins. Consequently, to give voice to the ways that Black women have navigated and survived the doctoral journey in a predominately white space, is nothing short of radical.

I first met Dr. Brittany Anderson when she interviewed for a position at the university where I had been working, and where she was ultimately hired as an assistant professor, my colleague, and program area partner. She began her interview with a story of a little Black girl, whose picture was placed on the screen, donning bangs, a red bow in her hair, and a red shawl, as was customary of the time. She described all the proclivities of this little girl—she was *"gifted."* Dr. Anderson introduced her research by telling her own story of how schools often bypass Black children's giftedness. It was a rare moment for me to hear a scholar talk about Black children's gifts, instead of centering their supposed shortcomings.

DOI: 10.4324/9781003292180-11

Dr. Anderson honed in on the ways how giftedness shows up for Black children, but also how it is dismissed, and even criminalized.

In meeting Dr. Anderson fairly early in my career as an assistant professor, I was immediately struck by the ways in which her presence in the space enriched my own experience as an assistant professor at a historically white institution. I was the only Black woman tenure-track professor in my department, and so I was always looked upon with suspicion as most of my colleagues kept a careful distance. However, when Dr. Anderson joined our team, I was able to experience a renewed sense of purpose, joy, and passion in my work. I no longer felt like an anomaly; continually pushing to perfect our equity-centered program, and working to engage in rigorous research in a department where little research external to the institution was happening. Like the stories in this book, I had a chance to experience the synergistic energy of gifted Blackgirlness personified. It was through our numerous, long conversations about our lives, our research, and the contested space that we occupied in the academy, that Dr. Anderson shared the desire that she, Dr. Richardson, and others had to tell their story of gifted/high-achieving Black women. The stories included the ways that tehse women, who were formally gifted/high-achieving Black girls, worked to support each other through their doctoral studies. I soon came to learn the Blackgirl energy that Dr. Anderson brought with her, and the way in which she encouraged me and helped me to embrace my own identity as gifted/high-achieving, had its roots in a community that had been cultivated over the course of her doctoral journey.

In my own experience as a Black woman who demonstrated intellectual gifts very early in life, it was refreshing to hear about other Black women who had begun to own their identities as gifted/high-achieving, and who chose to center Black women and girls, and their giftedness in their work. I had always been challenged by my giftedness. At the age of seven, I started taking the Q22 City bus in Far Rockaway, Queens in New York City. The closest school with a gifted program was miles away and did not offer a school bus route near my home. Despite all the changes my parents went through to get me enrolled in this school, I still was not admitted to the gifted program. In fact, several years later, my fourth grade teacher chastised me in front of the entire class for writing an essay that was exceptionally done. She claimed I had plagiarized the assignment. *My giftedness had been contested terrain.* It wasn't until middle school that I was admitted to my school's advanced program, where I completed the eighth and ninth grades in one year, and as a result, I graduated high school and entered college at 16 years old.

For me, my giftedness was unsettled territory. As a gifted/high-achieving Black girl in college, I was seen as an anomaly by peers and professors at my historically white institution. I have too many memories of times when my peers chose not to work with me in groups or refused to take my input on group assignments because of what they thought I *did not know*, yet, I most often surpassed them in classes, leaving them stunned. Still, there is so much unresolved trauma surrounding my identity as a gifted/high-achieving Black girl. I still grimace when I think about how schools, run by mostly white teachers, create barriers for Black girls and women to show up and thrive—a trend that continues through graduate and professional education.

My story further illustrates, as the authors' stories did, the complexities and challenges Black gifted/high-achieving women and girls must navigate as a baseline, but also in addition to the complexities wrought by their other intersectional identities, such as immigrant status, exceptionalities, motherhood, and racial identity, to name a few. These stories are immensely important to share because they demonstrate that more often than not, the problem is *them* (purveyors of the institution) not *us* (oppressed and minoritized groups). Disparities are maintained by a system that would rather see our gifts go to waste than have to contend with the brilliance Black women and girls have to offer the world. However, more than giving voice to the stories of gifted/high-achieving Black girls, this book contextualizes the power and synergy created when Black women come together in community to both support one another, but also embrace and grow the talents and epistemological inclinations of Black women. This work allows Black women to stake claim to their lived realities and declare that *just "for us"* is just enough. This book is an ode to the future of Black women and girls, it is and a roadmap to ways we can get free, even as we navigate the strictures of the historically white academy. This book shows us the power in reminding ourselves and each other of who we are and what we can accomplish—*together*.

ABOUT THE EDITORS

Brittany N. Anderson, Ph.D., is an Assistant Professor of Urban Education in Middle, Secondary, and K–12 Education (MDSK) at the University of North Carolina at Charlotte. Her research focuses on pre-service and in-service teacher development related to the talent development and identification of minoritized youth. Dr. Anderson's research also centers on the lived experiences of gifted Black girls and women, with an emphasis on their academic and social-emotional needs. Her grant work focuses on university-school-community partnerships that situate STEM engagement through critical and culturally relevant experiential learning development with high-ability Black girls, their teachers, and families. Through this work, she was recently named a 2022 National Science Foundation (NSF) CAREER fellow. For the past several years, Dr. Anderson has been involved in the professional learning of in-service teachers in urban schools, focused on anti-racist and culturally responsive teaching, STEM, and gifted education. Dr. Anderson was the 2017 recipient of the National

Association of Gifted Children (NAGC) Doctoral Award, NAGC's Special Populations 2022 Early Career Award, and the University of Georgia's COE 2023 Early Career Researcher Award.

Shaquinta L. Richardson, Ph.D., is a Life Coach and Owner of Beyond Achieving, LLC Coaching and Consulting where she supports the lives and careers of high-achieving Black women. Dr. Richardson is also a retired licensed therapist, supervisor, and clinical professor. During her time in academia, Dr. Richardson's research centered on the experiences of Black American women with intellectual and developmental disabilities within the family context and the influence of racial and gender identity on systemic experiences. Dr. Richardson has a Bachelor of Science in Marketing from Claflin University, a Master's in Marriage and Family Therapy from Converse College, and a Ph.D. in Human Development and Family Science with a Specialization in Marriage and Family Therapy and Disability Studies from The University of Georgia.

ABOUT THE CONTRIBUTORS

Funlola Are, Ph.D. is an assistant professor in the Faillace Department of Psychiatry and Behavioral Sciences. She earned her Ph.D. in clinical psychology at the University of Georgia and completed a clinical psychology doctoral internship and postdoctoral fellowship at the Medical University of South Carolina. Her program of research focuses on innovative methods to identify children at risk for traumatic stress and ways to expand the reach of evidence-based prevention and intervention initiatives to underserved populations. Pursuant to this, she has led and collaborated on investigations related to examining physical and biological factors related to socioemotional functioning in mother-child dyads, novel approaches to maltreatment identification in primary care settings, the dissemination and implementation of evidence-based trauma interventions, and the evaluation of an evidence-based kinship caregiver case management and maltreatment prevention program. She is a NIMH *Child Health Intervention, Prevention, and Services* Training Fellow and NICHD *Researchers in Child Abuse and Neglect* Training Fellow. She serves on the *Child Maltreatment* Editorial Board and is an ad-hoc reviewer for several journals in her field. She also serves as a member of the American Psychological Association, Society for Research in Child Development, and the Society for Implementation Research Collaborative.

Taryrn T.C. Brown, Ph.D., (she/her/hers) is an Assistant Professor in the Teachers, Schools, and Society program and the Program Coordinator for the Schools, Society, and Policy Specialization in Education Sciences at the University of Florida. Her program of research has three major foci: the

DOI: 10.4324/9781003292180-13

intersection of gender, race, and class in the lives of Black women and girls in and out of educational contexts; the amplification of Black women and girls' voices in prevention science; and the role parents, schools, and communities play in Black girls' socialization, literacies, and identity construction. With research at the nexus of Black Girlhood Studies and Black feminist thought, her work leverages various theoretical foundations (e.g., Black feminist theory, ecological systems theory; Black girl literacies; and Black girl cartography) and critical qualitative methodologies (e.g. youth participatory action research; photovoice; photo elicitation; and critical autoethnography). Dr. Brown is also the founder of the Black Girlhood Collaborative, a collective space for research, teaching, and learning in Black girlhood.

Joan Collier, Ph.D., is a scholar-practitioner of higher education and student affairs administration. Dr. Collier currently serves as Assistant Vice President for Equity and Inclusion at Rutgers University where she co-leads university-wide strategic plan implementation through comprehensive cross-campus engagement efforts to realize the university's commitment to fostering an inclusive learning and working environment. Dr. Collier is an Affiliate Faculty of the Graduate School of Education at Rutgers-New Brunswick, serves on the Editorial Board for the Journal of Diversity in Higher Education, and is co-founder of #CiteASista, a Black feminist project advocating for the inclusion, crediting, and centering of Black womxn's work within and beyond the academy.

Megan Hicks, Ph.D., is an Assistant Professor at Wayne State University in the School of Social Work and CEO/Founder of Hicks Data Consulting, LLC. Dr. Hicks is passionate about prevention/intervention work with Black communities, specifically focusing on health risk behaviors and juvenile justice outcomes. Her work investigates adverse childhood experiences (ACEs), community risk factors, and relational protective factors that impact health youth development. Currently, she is the principal investigator on multiple CDC-funded projects to create protective environments in schools through policy development. Additionally, she is evaluating the juvenile justice system in a Michigan county to decrease youth involvement in the criminal/legal system. Additionally, Dr. Hicks has expertise in program evaluation, prevention science, and community education. She also works with local non-profit organizations through her business, Hicks Data Consulting LLC, to provide curriculum development, program evaluation, and technical assistance. Lastly, she has a strong passion for working with the community and has received a Servant Leader Award through her community collaboration with the Detroit Phoenix Center.

Miranda Hill, Ph.D., MPH is a social scientist who combines interdisciplinary science with community-based participatory methods to examine the social and structural determinants of health inequities among marginalized populations. Her journey in women's health promotion first began over ten years ago with coordinating a mobile reproductive health clinic and developing health education workshops for diverse groups of underserved women. She has since allied with community-based organizations, gatekeepers, and academic and government researchers to conduct innovative and culturally responsive projects with the common goal of promoting social justice in population health. Dr. Hill is also an exercise and meditation enthusiast who enjoys traveling and experiencing new adventures with her family and friends.

Elizabeth Farrah Louis, Ph.D., is a Haitian-American clinical psychologist at Harvard Medical School where she provides therapy to patients of Haitian heritage and other diverse populations and engages in research. She has experience providing clinical services to refugees, asylum seekers, and survivors of torture from Latin America, the Caribbean, Africa, and Asia. Dr. Louis also conducts therapy with children and adolescents and collaborates with social services and organizations for optimal forms of wellness. Dr. Louis has a history of serving diverse religious and spiritual entities, groups, and underrepresented students in various academic institutions. Since 2015, Dr. Louis has been engaged in extensive community-based work in Haiti focused on trauma, disaster relief, research, and mental health. She is a recipient of several awards, including the U.S. State Department's Boren Fellowship where she lived in Haiti (2017–2018) and worked with Zanmi Lasanté/Partners in Health to address self-care, mental health literacy, gender-based violence, and child development. She also completed the National Institutes of Health's Fogarty Global Health Fellowship with Partners in Health/Inshuti Mu Buzima in Rwanda (2019–2020) where she supported mental health service delivery and research initiatives. Dr. Louis serves on national and international boards with a focus on supporting and empowering underserved populations.

Jillian A. Martin, Ph.D. (She/Her/Hers), is currently a Fulbright U.S. Scholar to Ghana where she is doing teaching and research at the University of Cape Coast. Prior to her current role, Dr. Martin served in various higher education capacities (civic and community engagement, assessment and evaluation, housing and residence life, student activities, and diversity initiatives). She focuses her scholar-practice on creating opportunities for the use of inquiry (assessment, evaluation, and research) in intentional practice. Her research agenda includes: student athlete transitions, socialization of student affairs professionals, and student services in higher education within a Ghanaian context and epistemological pathways, case study design, and survey design. Her dissertation research explores student services at a liberal arts institution in Ghana focusing on the implications of assessment practices with a student services unit at a Ghanaian institution. Dr. Martin has extensive research and practice in Ghana. She continues to present regionally and nationally while contributing to scholarship through publications. She received her Ph.D. and M.Ed. in College Student Affairs Administration from the University of Georgia and her B.S. in Biopsychology from Oglethorpe University.

INDEX

acting white phenomenon 22, 26
adinkra symbolism 33, 42–3
African American 2, 68, 112–13; Great Migration of 99; history classes 74; musical legacies 32; schooling 21–2; Studies 16
African American Cultural Center 55
African American Vernacular English (AAVE) 28
Allen, E. 4
Anderson, B. N. 9, 122–3, 131–2; academic expectations 20–1; creating spaces with other Black women 26; family socialization 18–21; gender identity 19–20, 26–7; gifted blackgirlhood narratives 24–5; graduate experience 23–4; K–12 21–2; navigating doctoral experience as first-generation 27–8; schooling experiences 21–5; sexuality and shaming 25; undergraduate 22–3
Angelou, M. 33
anti-blackness 16, 50, 99, 131
anxiety 15, 27, 39, 41, 128
Asian American 61

belonging 24, 27, 56, 84, 122; to community 46–8, 56; Endarkened Feminist Epistemology in 48; framework for 48; peer-group 23; sense of 3, 47–50, 52–4, 89

biracial identity 3, 74; development 71–3; at Predominately White Institution 76–7; suggestions for navigating PWI 80–1; Trayvon's murder and 77–80
Black Girl Magic 80, 113; at Predominately White Graduate Institution 75–6
Black Student Association 74
Black women and girls 20, 55–6, 58, 83–7, 106, 131–3; #CiteASista 53–4; academic support 28–9; blogging community 54; boundaries, establishing 125–6; building community with other 128–9; College Student Affairs Administration 48–9; create spaces for other black women 25–6; in doctoral programs 3–5; Endarkened Feminist Epistemology 47–8; family socialization of 12–14, 18–21; fear, disrupting 126–7; gifted/high-achieving 1, 5, 11–12, 24, 122–3 (*see also* gifted Black women and girls); maternal health inequities among 108; navigating doctoral experience as first-generation 27–30; navigating doctoral process 111, 118, 120–1; perfectionism 129; schooling experiences of 14–18, 21–5; self-care 124; self-trust 126–7; Sista-Scholars and Sista

Circles 50–3; social support 29–30; tools and strategies to protection and restoration of 123
boundaries 23, 96, 108, 129; establishing 125–6; fragile 19; setting 126
Boylorn, R. M. 10, 11, 84
Brown, B. 33
Butler, O. E. 33

Chang, G. 85
Cite A Sista (CAS) 53–4
Cobb-Roberts, D. 4–5
Cohambee River Collective 54
collective writing energy 28, 29
College Student Affairs Administration (CSAA) program 48–9, 54
Collins, P. H. 33, 76–7, 84, 85, 86–7, 93
colonialism 42, 49
communication 20, 33, 112, 115, 126; with advisors 80; in formal spaces 80; overcommunication 81; personal 51, 56
Cooper, A. J. 36
COVID-19 pandemic 95, 118, 124
Crenshaw, K. 33
critical thinking 16, 20, 23, 34, 68
cultural identity and 87

depression 41, 73, 79
Dillard, C. B. 1, 33, 42–3, 49–50, 87
disasters 3, 6, 131; earthquake in Haiti 114–15; Hurricane Matthew 116–17
discrimination 54, 62; gender 61; racial 72–3, 78; realities of 60; systemic 66
distress 116; financial 124
distrust 14

Elementary and Secondary Education Act 10
Endarkened Feminist Epistemology (EFE) 2, 42, 47–8, 50
equity 51, 84, 99, 106, 132
equity/inequities 18, 21, 51, 69, 84, 99, 106; -centered program 132; maternal health 108
Esnard, T. 4–5
exceptionally gifted Black women and girls 32–3, 43–4

family socialization 3, 10, 11, 12–14, 18–21, 25–6
fear 17, 89, 90; of being back 127; of being taunted and teased 100; disrupting 126–7; of doing wrong thing 128; of failure 27, 101, 127, 128; of getting in trouble 100; of losing 128; -mongering 25; motherhood and 108; of not meeting milestones 110; of setting boundaries 126
feminism 2, 4, 6, 9, 47, 48, 51, 54, 84–5
Forcey, L. 85
Franklin, A. J. 4
Free Application for Federal Student Aid 63

Gates Millennium Scholarship 63
gender 2, 5–6, 10, 36, 47, 51, 118, 123; cisgender 111; differences 112–13; discourses 83; discrimination 61; identity 11, 12, 13–14, 19–20, 94; nuances of partnership 29; racism and 4, 23, 25, 71, 127; roles 85, 112; shaming 25; socialization 12, 25; violence 46
Ghana Study Abroad in Education 50
gifted Black women and girls 26–7, 36, 40, 42, 46–8, 131–3; biracial 74–6, 80, 81; emerging gifts 100–1; exceptionally 32–3, 43–4; first-generation American 58–61; first-generation student 10–11, 17, 20, 22, 27–30; gifted gaze for 1–3; motherscholar identity (see motherscholar identity); purpose and rationale 5–6; self-care 124
giftedness 6, 14, 25, 73, 81, 101, 122–3; children's 131–2; defined 10; see also gifted Black women and girls
Glenn, E. 85
Graduate and Professional Scholars (GAPS) 76, 77, 78

Haitian Creole 111–12, 114–15, 117–19; disaster work, engaged in 117–18; distance 114–15; facing tragedy with courage 115–17; Haitian girl, identity 111–14; sacred communal or familial yard 120–1; strong woman 118–19
Haynes, C. 4

health risk behaviors 81
Hill, L. 32–3, 35–6, 40–3, 83
Hispanic population 21–2
Historically Black Colleges and Universities (HBCUs) 15
homeplace 10, 83–5, 96–7, 123; defined 91; motherscholar 91–3; (other) homeplaces 91; resilience and embodied motherwork in 95–6
hooks b., 51, 85, 91
Hurricane Matthew 116–17

imposter syndrome 23, 39, 101–2, 105, 119; battling 27; ways for mitigating 24
intersectionality theory 5, 6, 9, 33, 106–8
isolation 41, 68, 85, 124, 125; in embodying motherwork 91; feelings of 29, 39, 73; free from 30; minimizing 53

Jordan, J. 5

Lacy, M. 52, 56
Latinx population 21–2, 113
liberation 3, 10, 24, 54, 73, 104–6, 123; commitment to 51; -focused politic 51; opportunity for 33
Lorde, A. 30, 33, 52
love 48, 51, 55, 87–8, 116; benefits and trade-offs of 106–8; of learning 22, 34; themes of 36; of working 23
Love, B. L. 56

maladaptive coping mechanism 23, 27, 122, 128; *see also* perfectionism
malnutrition 110, 124
marginality 47–8
Marley, Zion David 83
marriage 3, 17, 68, 85–7, 90–1, 106–10
Martin, Trayvon 77–8
Matias, C. 84
mattering 47–8, 49, 85–7, 89
mental health 6, 41, 66, 72–3, 112, 116, 125; accountability 10; counseling 114; and crisis response experience 114–15; disaster work 114; Haitian 117; international work 115; research in Rwanda 118
mentoring 4, 6, 52, 53, 65, 69, 80, 86–90, 95, 102, 114–15

microaggressions 17, 23, 66, 71, 119
migrantion/immigrantion 12, 58, 59, 61–2, 67, 69, 111–12, 133
miseducation 32–3, 43–4, 83; aware of 42; educator 38–40; post-secondary 38; primary and secondary school 35–8; unlearning 40–2
motherhood/mothering 3, 83–4, 90, 94–6; defined 85; discourses on 85; fear and 108; and home, expectations of 89; isolation in 91; reprioritization and extension 108–10; socialized negotiations of 85
motherscholar identity 3, 83–4, 90, 94–6; autoethnography 84–5; framework 90; homeplace 91–3; mentoring 90; resilience 95–6
Multicultural Services and Programs (MSP) 55

National Academy Foundation program 22
National Honor Society 73
neocolonialism 42
Nicolas, G. 114–15
Nigerian American 58–60
Norris, J. 11

Ohio State University (OSU) 73–4
overcommunication 81

people-pleasing personality 20, 25
perfectionism 20, 22–3, 24–5, 27, 39, 43, 122, 128
physical survival 87, 93–5
power 51, 133; of belonging and community 55; empowerment 12, 26, 54, 56, 78–9, 87, 94, 110; reclamation of 95; structures 5, 103; of voice 84
Predominately White Institution (PWI) 3, 10, 22, 29, 71, 75, 107, 114; being biracial at 76–7, 80–1; intrinsic drive as tool in 101–2; in Kansas 103; resilience, coping, and black liberation in 104–6; survival politics in 102–6
pregnancy 13, 88–90, 108–9, 112; teenage 25; *see also* motherhood/mothering
Pre-Med track 38, 65, 103
Psychological First Aid (PFA) 116

Index

racial awareness 78
racial discrimination 72–3, 78
racial identity 23–4, 49, 94, 113, 133; development 22, 71–4; Trayvons murder and 78; *see also* biracial identity
racial representation 105
racial resilience 91
racial socialization 60, 72, 74
racial tension 19, 95
racial violence, coping with 99–100
racism 2–5, 10, 12, 15–22, 27, 47, 51, 62, 113, 118, 123, 30,36; avoiding 61; College Student Affairs Administration and 49; cultural identity and 87; discourses 83; endemic intersectional 101; exclusion 55; gendered 4, 23, 25, 71, 127; to giftedness 101; making 64; minority 65; realities of 60; sexism 4; structural 122; systemic 4, 66, 122
relearning 33, 44; authenticity 43–4; with others 43; and (re)membering 42–3
(re)membering 46, 85–7; framework for 48 (*see also* Endarkened Feminist Epistemology (EFE)); learning to 49–50; relearning and 42–3
resilience 2, 104–6; Ayiti 115; level of 127; motherscholar 95–6; in PWI educational settings 104–6; racial 91
Richardson, S. 9, 123–4, 131–2; academic expectations 14; family socialization 12–14; gender identity 13–14; graduate programs 16–18; K–12 14–15; schooling experiences 14–18; undergraduate 15–16
Rites of Passage (ROP) 55

Saint-Jean, F. 116
Sawyer, R. D. 11
Schlossberg, N. K. 47, 49
self-care 30, 52, 117–18; boundaries for 125–6; defined 124; ways to do 125
self-concept 71, 91
self-esteem 71, 73, 74, 120
self-talk, negative 41, 43
self-trust 43, 126–7
sexism 47; cissexism 54; endemic intersectional 101; racialized 4

sexuality 13, 25
shaming 13, 37, 52, 108; for being smart 26; gender 19, 25; old-fashioned 25
Sista Circles 6, 20, 24, 29, 51–3
Sista-Scholars 10, 46, 50–3, 56
sleep deprivation 90, 99, 110, 124, 125
social awareness 78
socialization 2; early education and 59–62; family 3, 10, 11, 12–14, 18–21, 25–6; to friendships and community with other women 25; gendered 12, 25; graduate 48; implications of 91; negotiations of motherhood 85; for professionals 42; racial 60, 72, 74; white 72
Social support 29–30, 41, 43, 65–6
Socioeconomic Status (SES) 123
stereotype threat 23, 27, 39
Stewart, S. 4
Strayhorn, T. L. 47
stress 40, 42, 117, 124; distress 116, 124
systemic racism 4, 66, 122

Tawwab, N. 126
threats 126; death 72; stereotype 23, 27, 39
TRIO program 113
Trump, Donald 78, 79
trust 26, 119, 121, 126; distrust 14; God 120; self-trust 43, 126–7

unlearning 26, 33, 44, 49, 51, 54; coping mechanisms 41; impacts of 42; miseducation 40–2

violence 115; epistemological 48; gendered 46; ontological 48; racial 99–100; racialized 46; structural 48, 56
vulnerability 11, 33, 93–5, 105, 115

Walker, A. 33
White people 3–4, 13–15, 23, 26, 60, 78, 114–18, 131–3; being socialized as 72; -dominated space 79, 93; schooling 21–2; supremacy 50, 53, 56, 127; *see also* Predominately White Institution (PWI)
Williams, B. 53
Winkle-Wagner, R. 29
Woodson, C. G. 32, 33, 36

Printed and bound by CPI Group (UK) Ltd, Croydon, CR0 4YY
01/12/2024
01797780-0004